To My Sister - Rashma

PURAN SINGH - A LIFE SKETCH

*With Love
Simran*

The sculpture reproduced on the endpaper depicts a scene where three soothsayers are interpreting to King Suddhodana the dream of Queen Maya, mother of Lord Buddha. Below them is seated a scribe recording the interpretation. This is perhaps the earliest available pictorial record of the art of writing in India.

From : Nagarjunakonda, 2nd century A.D.
Courtesy : National Museum, New Delhi.

PURAN SINGH - A LIFE SKETCH

Maya Devi Puran Singh

Edited by : Mohinder Singh Randhawa
Translated by : Swinder Singh Uppal

Sahitya Akademi

SAHITYA AKADEMI

Rabindra Bhavan, 35, Ferozeshah Road, New Delhi 110 001.
Sales : 'Swati', Mandir Marg, New Delhi 110 001.
ADA Ranga Mandira 109 J.C. Road, Bangalore - 560 002.
23A/44X, Diamond Harbour Road, Calcutta 700 053.
"Guna Buildings" IInd Floor, 304-305 Anna Salai,
Teynampet, Madras - 600 018.
172, Mumbai Marathi Grantha Sangrahalaya Marg,
Dadar, Bombay 400 014.

ISBN 81-7201-395-7

© Sahitya Akademi
First Published 1993

Rs. 25/-

Published by the Sahitya Akademi, New Delhi and Printed by
Udayam Offsets, Madras.

Contents

1.	Rawalpindi	...	7
2.	Lahore	...	20
3.	Dohiwala	...	39
4.	Dehradun	...	52
5.	Patiala	...	66
6.	Gwalior	...	69
7.	Suraiya (Gorakpur)	...	79
8.	Sheikhupura	...	82

1. Rawalpindi

I was born in Rawalpindi in a pious family. My grandfather was Bhakat Jawahar Mal. People loved to call him 'Saiyan Sahib (Lord) Saint). He was a wine-contractor at Hajro. But he would advise whoever came to him to purchase wine, not to drink as it was injurious to health. Rather, he inspired them to the practice of spiritualism. In fact, many people foresook drinking and under his persuasion took to true Bhakti. This is how he earned the title of 'Bhakat' (Saint). While sitting at his shop, he used to recite and enjoy the singing of 'Heer Waris Shah'. People flocked to his shop to hear his melodious voice.

In our family there was a practice of remembering God regularly, reciting religious poetry and hearing theological discourses. From my childhood, I was regaled with many stories including those of 'Satis' (widows who burnt themselves to death on the death of their husbands). Of them, the tale of Parvati, haunted me forever, the way she had made up her mind to marry only Lord Shiva. From my childhood I used to worship Devi and Parvati. I was engaged to Puran Singh when I was hardly ten. Like Parvati I was determined to wed only Puran Singh and I felt peace and tranquillity in his devotion.

His parents had sent Puran Singh to Lahore for studies where we were also settled. He visited us often and on, and his rare qualities increased my devotion. He had a distinct manner of speaking and was handsome beyond description. I used to peep at him on the sly. We never confronted each other.

When my father expired, the entire family responsibilities fell on my elder brother Bhakat Sain Dass who was just twenty-one at that time. We were a very small family – two sisters and one brother. Bhakat Sain Dass was a man of strict principles and did not tolerate anything against the family tradition.

In 1900 there was a proposal to send two brilliant students to Japan for higher studies. Puran Singh who had not even completed his graduation was selected. The other was Damodar Singh, an elderly married man. To judge Puran Sigh's ability and fortitude a congregation was called in a gurudwara outside the city. The aspirants were asked to deliver an extempore speech on the qualities of unity. When Puran Singh's turn came he walked up to the dais and picked up a flower vase containing a cluster of flowers. Pointing towards the fully blossomed roses he said that their unison had added to their glitter and glamour; otherwise they would be reduced to petals worth nothing. And he went on to deliver an extempore speech for a full hour without faltering for a moment.

It was winter. The gurudwara was at about two and a half miles away from the city. S. Buta Singh, one of the Organisers, desired for someone to bring from his house his spectacles which he had forgotten to bring. Puran Singh volunteered to help. He was a very fast walker. When he returned back with the spectacles no one was ready to believe that he had fetched the spectacles from Buta Singh's house. They thought that someone had delivered him the spectacles somewhere on the way. But when it came to light that he had actually fetched the spectacles from his residence, he was selected for the foreign sojourn.

Before leaving for Japan, he came to the Golden Temple, Amritsar, to meet us all. We all were sitting in the balcony of a *Bunga* (residential abode.) He was heading towards us in a joyfully intoxicated mood. He had no beard, but he had allowed his hair to flow from his head downwards. Everybody felt rejoiced to see him. My nieces broke into a dance. When he came up the staircase, I hid myself, as per the social customs of the time. My mother embraced him and could not fight back her tears. She asked him in a faltering voice, "When do you hope to return? My daughter is of marriageable age. Had your father-in-law been alive today, he would not have allowed you to go abroad like this."

"I will be back soon. I will earn a lot for your daughter," Puran replied.

After reaching Japan, he was in regular correspondence with my elder brother Bhakat Sain Dass and would always entreat him for my education. He used to write twenty to twenty-five foolscap pages delineating the advantages of education and drawbacks of illiteracy (alas! that literature could not be saved from ruin).

Bhakat Sain Dass however, was not in favour of girls being educated. He used to say, "An uneducated woman can challenge a man but a literate woman can challenge even God." So he did not make any plans for my education.

During his stay in Japan Puran Singh suffered from a prolonged bout of typhoid. To save him, the doctors had to shave off his hair, after consulting Damodar Singh and some others. After recovering from typhoid, he left studies and began giving lectures on freedom. He even started an English paper by the name of *Buddering Dawn*. The avowed policy of the paper was to expose the inhuman cruelties and excesses of the English people in India. The English people must be turned out from the Indian soil. He returned to India with this very purpose. The Japanese generously aided on him; they would secretly leave money in the rickshaw in which he travelled. In one of his saintly sojourns, he met Swami Ram Tirath and was so much enamoured of him that he became a *sanyasi* (ascetic) and took to donning saffron clothes.

Puran-Sanyasi wrote to my brother Bhakat Sain Dass "I have become a *sanyasi*. You are free to marry your sister elsewhere."

During the whole day Bhakat Sain Dass did not give the slightest hint to any one. But late at night he enquired of my mother, "Is Maya asleep?" My mother replying in the affirmative asked, "What is the matter?" Since marriage preparations were afoot in our house, he cautiously leaked out the whole secret to her.

On hearing my mother began to tremble as if under a spell. She started uttering, "Waheguru Waheguru" (Oh! God). My mother was certain that her daughter Maya, a disciple of Gori deity, would not even like to listen to the proposal of marrying any other person.

Bhakat Sain Dass proposed certain names to her for my marriage. I was wide awake and spoke aloud, "I was married to him the day my father had performed the engagement ceremony. I have been worshipping him all these years. I cannot even dream of marrying any other person. If you force me to do that, I will either jump from the roof or pour kerosene oil on myself and burn myself alive."

My brother was stunned when he heard this. Next day he wrote a letter to Puran Singh's parents at Abbotabad of Puran Singh's letter saying, "We have received a letter from Puran Singh in which he has informed us that he has become a *sanyasi* and we are free to marry our sister to any one else. But my sister is adamant to marry only Puran Singh and none else. We are helpless. Kindly ask your son to come back to India." He had enclosed a copy of Puran Singh's letter.

This shocking news paralysed Puran's family. Puran Singh was actually at that time in Calcutta having returned to India.

Infatuated by parental love, his parents immediately decided to undertake the railway journey to Calcutta in spite of the fact that they had never travelled even as far as up to Amritsar by rail. Fortunately, in Calcutta they were able to trace the whereabouts of their son. When his mother saw him clad in saffron clothes, she clung to him and wept bitterly. His father was exceedingly enraged and shouted, "Is this the earning you have brought for us?" But his mother did not loosen her embrace and clung to him.

Next morning, when Puran Singh enquired from his mother the well-being of the other family members, she lamented, "Dear son, I have left the entire family and have rushed here to meet you. Your sister Ganga is pregnant and is expecting any day. But I didn't bother about all that and have come rushing to you. Ganga also insisted that I should go and meet you. Your marriage preparations are completed on both sides and marriage songs are on our lips. Ganga has commissioned me to take you to her so that she could meet you alive at least once in her life. Kindly accompany me for her sake, meet your sister Ganga and then you will be free to decide your future. I won't stand in your way."

Lalaji, his father, was however still very much enraged. "How will I face the people around me because of your misdeed?"

His mother admonished her husband, "how dare you scold him who has brightened the name of his forefathers?" She was under constant fear that her son might refuse to accompany them, being rebuked by his father. She kept on insisting, "You meet your sister at least once. She is on her death bed." As in his childhood she could induce him to act according to her wishes, so now by touching upon his sentiments she was successful in luring him to accompany them. His mother thanked God Almighty when they all boarded the train to Abbotabad. The mother and son sat together but the grudging father took a separate seat.

After a few day's rail journey, the mother along with her *sanyasi* son reached Abbotabad. Seeing Puran in saffron clothes, people flocked around him. Puran walked ahead followed by his mother and public at large. Hearing that their beloved brother was coming to meet them, both his sisters — Ganga and Lajan — came out to greet their loving brother. Both the sisters clasped their brother to their bosoms and wept bitterly. But the eyes of their brother which used to shed tears at the slightest emotional touch, remained dry and not a single drop of tear came out of them. Puran Singh remained repentant throughout his life for this lapse on his part.

The whole family was deeply attached to him and could not bear to see him in saffron. At every step, they would bewail and weep bitterly as if in distress. It is difficult to describe the touching scene when the whole family met *Sanyasi* Puran.

Ganga was blessed with a son, but she developed fever with high temperature following the delivery. Puran Singh was by her side all the time. Looking deep into her sparkling eyes, he enquired, "What is your earnest wish?" "Please give me a solemn pledge that you will marry the girl you have been engaged with." The moment he nodded in the affirmative, Ganga's soul left her perishable body and settled in peace.

Puran frankly told his mother, "I will marry the girl only after meeting her."

The elite at Abbotabad gave Puran Singh his due respect and honour. Barrister Babu Parma Nand performed the change-in ceremony (abdication of saffron clothes and donning of worldly clothes). Since his father and grandfather could not bear those saffron clothes, these were burnt to ashes much against the wishes of Puran's mother.

At that time our family was away at Peshawar as the dreaded disease plague was rampant in Rawalpindi. My mother-in-law wrote to Bhakat Sain Dass that she would be coming to meet him along with her son Puran Singh. 'Puran Singh has been insisting that he will give his final decision about the marriage only after meeting the girl.'

Bhakat Sain Dass was not agreeable to this proposal. "How can he be allowed to meet Maya before marriage?" He was very much enraged and annoyed. He wrote back "I cannot permit it."

When Puran Singh read this letter he told his mother," the matter is settled. I cannot marry her without a prior meeting." The mother persuaded him to accompany her with the promise of arranging their secret meeting without the knowledge of her brother.

His mother brought her son to Peshawar. When they reached our house, I was in a precarious and undescribable state of mind, trembling from head to toe. My heart beat had increased and I was all mute. Till then I had never come face to face with my mother-in-law. Suddenly she stepped into my room and whispered to me "Puran is coming to meet you. Meet him with full confidence and courtesy. Don't hide yourself."

He entered the room where I was standing. I was trembling all over. He said, "I am a recluse. Marry me only if you are prepared to become a mendicant; at times you may have to beg."

"I am ready to do anything for you. I don't need anything except your goodself," was my humble reply.

"Alright, then accompany me right now," he said commandingly. "I am the grand-daughter of a very high family. Please excuse me for this. After marriage I will be entirely at your disposal. You may make me a mendicant or anything else. Obedience to you will be my primary duty." I said all this in a determined but courteous manner.

We could exchange only these notes. I was happy that I would lead the life of a mendicant visiting many hearths and homes. But alas, that never happened.

At that time a song haunted me, which I used to sing since my childhood.

> We are like a roaming recluse, difficult it will be to
>   forget us.   A speared man may live some moments but slayed with eyebrow sharpened-arrows,
>   it is difficult to forget.

I thought he was, perhaps, a victim of some sharpened eyebrows and will, in turn, make me his own victim, transforming me into a mendicant. In fact, all our life, our home was a centre for recluses. People had composed many songs about him, but I, now, remember only one couplet.

> Awake, awake, oh! sleeping Puran
> Maya entreats you through whistles

My cousin Bhakat Narain Dass was a Sessions Judge in Kashmir. He had a great liking for Puran Singh from his childhood. He desired that Puran Singh should wear long hair and beard before wedding, so that guests might not make stories about him. With this purpose and with a view to introduce him to His Highness the Maharaja of Kashmir, he invited Puran Singh to Kashmir. Puran Singh accepted his invitation. When Bhakat Narain Dass introduced Puran Singh to His Highness, he bestowed on him the Role of Honour. In Kashmir, Puran Singh delivered many lectures enunciating the need for installing industries all over India. Bhakat Narain Dass took special interest in entertaining him and courteously persuaded him to wear long hair and beard to which request he acceded.

When he came back and told this to his mother who was known for her fearlessness and straightforwardness. She felt as if her self-respect and integrity had been injured. She openly declared, "I don't want that you should wear long hair and beard under somebody's coercion or under the pressure of family's misgivings." His mother was intoxicated with joy and pride that her son had come back after getting higher education from abroad and was going to be married very shortly. She vehemently and openly announced, "I consider only those people as my relatives who are prepared to share in our joy rather than raise pre-conditions to have their final say in the matter."

When it came to be known that Puran Singh would be married with shorn hair, many stories and misgivings shot up in our family. Who would like to join the marriage of a fallen Sikh? After a great deal of consideration most of the people from both sides decided to boycott the entire marriage ceremony and none would join the marriage procession.

Our family relations with many people were like the embroidering knots in the woven strings of a cot.

Even S. Teja Singh, husband of my sister-in-law, Lajan, wrote to her, "Please come back immediately. If you want to stay on with your fallen Sikh brother, you may stay there for the rest of your life. I will have nothing to do with you."

Lajan did not respond to her husband's letter and participated in the wedding of her brother's marriage with full vigour and joy.

Bhakat Sain Dass, in consultation with Bhakat Narain Dass directed the *Pandit* (religious priest) to finalise the marriage date which was fixed for March 4, 1904 and all the relatives were informed accordingly. When Bhakat Narain Dass came from Kashmir to attend our marriage, he was not aware of the fact that Puran Singh had not started keeping long hair and beard. Next day when they met he was shocked to see him still with shorn hair. He said, "You have degraded yourself in my eyes by not fulfilling your promise."

Swami Puran replied, "When I was coming out of your house, I found a broom lying down in the way. I picked it up and brought it with me. With the help of that broom I have swept away all the good counsels you were kind enough to offer me."

My father-in law had great respect for Pandit Bhagwan Dass, who was known for his religious austerity, yogic achievements and miraculous feats. For the uninterrupted completion of our marriage, he had started Durga recitations eight days in advance. Many respectable citizens were to join the marriage procession. There were about hundred participants. The decorations were made on such a grand scale and with such lavishness that it looked as though it were the marriage-procession of a prince. The mare on which the bridegroom was to sit was profusely adorned. The saffron coloured turban affixed with aigrette had doubly added to the handsomeness of the bridegroom. Though there was a social boycott, even then hundreds of people thronged on their roof-tops to have a glimpse of the marriage procession. When the procession reached our house girls in their gorgeous dresses and ornaments rushed to see the handsome *sanyasi* in the garb of a bridegroom, performing the weddingrites. Though the bridegroom was known to be an obstinate, yet his obstinacy could not stand the tide of sentiments expressed by his sisters-in-law.

As per custom I had to come out to put the Jaimala (wedding garland) around the groom's neck. My friends assisted in bringing me to him. I was trembling with a terrible nervousness. My hands looked crimson with the use of myrtle, my arms bedecked with red bangles and on my head was a red cloth. Having looked constantly at the burning earthen-lamps even my eyes had turned red. With a feeling of dejection, my lifeless benumbed body was walking only with the assistance of my friends. A Jaimala garland was handed over to my trembling hands and I was asked by my friends to garland him and then bend down in his honour. But the moment I bent down my head, he gently touched me and prevented me from bending further. I could not get again in my whole life that feeling of electrifying touch which I was fortunate to experience at that moment. That stirring ecstasy affected the whole of my body as is done by a little stone thrown in the still waters of a pond.

Garlanding over, my girl friends took me back to my earlier seat and leaving me there, they surrounded the bridegroom. A lot of bantering followed. They asked him to recite some *chhand* (poetic couplets) saying, "Your unscrupulous mother does not seem to have trained you for this. You consider yourself to be a fine and intelligent man, but we will accept your intelligence only when you get through our test."

All the girls had encircled him and were not giving him a chance to utter a word. By that time his mother, sister and other relatives had entered the room and came to his rescue. His mother very much elated when she found her son encircled by his young sisters-in-law, she loudly addressed them all and said, "Oh bewitching sisters-in-law, you have surrounded my innocent son all around. Be patient and listen to his couplets."

They retorted, "Now you have come to assist him. Why, doesn't he know how to speak?"

His mother persuaded him to recite some poetic couplets and he recited the following:-

> I am not in a mood to spin the spinning wheel.
> Oh mother, do not bind the broken threads for spinning,
> The very sight of the spinning wheel baffles me
> How dare I sit amongst my friends?

The pangs of life have wringed out my blood
And my whole flesh is without a drop of it
Oh Hussain, bewitched in love, are devoid of sense,
And at last wise counsellors feel baffled and helpless.

(2)

It is easy to die on a burning pyre
One has just to determine and jump in it.

But too difficult is to play the game of love,
Pathetically one dies bit by bit in it.

But by taking an intoxicant
One is able to win over the ailments of this and the other world.

(3)

Oh Saint with Contentment, Beauty and Knowledge
You have to win over the Beautiful

Oh friends, Almighty, clear your minds from all enmity,
If you want to have a bath in Love

With bathed body and purified mind
Your flower-blossomed face looks attractive,

My glow is like the burning fire,
Life flows like a stream, it is not a dream or an imitation

The appeal of male to the female
Is identical with Cuckoo, Nightingale, Crow and Dog

(4)

Walking aside from God's creations
Is like cracking the wooden pipkin,

By crumbling down the fragile petal,
You have pushed away the cloak of worship

I am a witness to this feat
Of having met the God Almighty.

After hearing these poetic couplets, the girls dragged him to the room where I was sitting near the marriage pitcher. Many earthen lamps of mustard oil were burning brightly. The girls surrounded him and demanded *Lachi* (cardomon) and *Laung* (cloves). But his mother had forgotten to provide him with cardomon. Finding him caught in this critical situation, the girls started singing:

> Provide us with cardomon and clove
> Or hand over your real aunts to us.
>
> Provide us with cloves and betel nut
> Or hand over to us your unmarried sister.
>
> Provide us with cloves
> Or hand over to us your married sister.

One girl taunted him saying, "Oh friends, bring pearls for him to string, we have to be sure whether he can see at night." Some girls brought some undrilled pearls. The bridegroom tried to string those pearls but failed every time. The girls started laughing and taunted, "His eye-sight seems to be defective."

His mother came to his rescue once again and whispered in his ears, "Drop down every pearl in the pretext of stringing them and demand for more." In this way all the pearls got exhausted.

Those Pothohari girls went on enjoying in this manner for some time. But I was sitting mute and still, unmindful of fun. At that moment I had neither any sense of belonging for anything nor any feeling of jubilation.

Subsequently all assembled there had their dinner and went way for taking rest. The marriage ceremony was to be performed at midnight. Banana poles had been erected on four sides of a patch of ground and in between was the pit for preserving the consecrated fire. I was asked to sit on a large seat made of reeds, where the bridegroom was already seated. Pandits were reciting certain Sanskrit slokas of which I could make any sense. Every now and then they put some *samagri* (material used at the time of a *hawan*) into our hands and asked us to pour the same into the fire when they uttered the word *sawaha*. My friends who were sitting beside me, at every nod of the Pandit, would take my hand full of *samagri* near the burning fire and help me pour on it. By then I was feeling completely exhausted and lifeless.

Then the Pandit recited a Sanskrit sloka and instructed my brother Bhakat Sain Dass to perform the *kanyadan* (gifting of a girl without any pecuniary gain). After performing this ceremony, my brother put my hand into the hand of Swami Puran. I had already entrusted my heart to him, but after giving him my hand I offered my mind and entire body to him. The unfamiliarity for him vanished and a sense of belonging came to me. I felt as if I had known him since many earlier births. Now he was my master and a sense of servitude for him crept into my mind.

We came to recognize each other in this resurgence again. Though I was not fully aware of my previous births, in the horoscope of Puran Singh it was stated that I had been his wife for the last three births and would remain so in future as well. Could be because I was in the habit of reciting this couplet (sloka) of Parvati since my childhood:

Give me births as many you like
But wed me only with Shambu and none else.

After I bid farewell to my people I was brought to his house in a palanquin. After the ceremonies were completed, everybody went to bed. Swamiji told his mother, 'I have fulfilled the promise given to Ganga. From tomorrow myself and Maya will become ascetics and leave this house forever."

"As you feel." His mother replied, "But I have to tell you something which I had not told you earlier. In your absence, I have been taking loans in the hope that you would pay them back after your return. We constructed this new house when you were aboad with the desire that you should grace it and enjoy your life by living here. I have kept all the multi-coloured pegs in the house covered with cloth, so that their colours do not fade away before your and Maya's use. These were my sincere and motherly sentiments. We owe Five thousand rupees to Seth Choohra Mal of Abottabad and Two thousand to S. Sant Singh. All your younger brothers had to be educated. What else could your old father and mother do? These uncared young children will have to roam the streets. You both will pass your days by begging, but what shall happen to us?"

All these revelations made the son ponder deeply. He realised that about seven thousand rupees loan had to be paid back to people.

I had been thinking during performance of all those marriage ceremonies, how my ascetic husband and I would go from door to door begging for our livelihood. All my ornaments and clothes got prepared for the marriage looked absurd to me.

But his mother had planned to get her son fully absorbed in domestic affairs. She was also under the impression that I would side with her. But, in fact, this was not the case. I had not developed any sense of belonging to anything except that of fulfilling the desires of my beloved husband. My mother-in-law was not happy.

Swamiji never compelled me to do anything. He always respected the labour of love. He was of the opinion that in every heart there burnt a fire of love. But it cannot be kindled unless it is aired with sentiments. If you are not able to find your companion upto your taste, you remain bewildered and empty within in spite of having treasures filled to the coffers. A man with sincere sentiments is always innocent and simple.

2. Lahore

In April 1904, I went to Koh Marri (Marri hills) with my parents. Bhakat Ishar Dass, elder brother of my cousin Narain Dass, requested Puran Singh to visit Lahore to deliver a few lectures on ' Essential Oils'. Puran readily agreed. At Lahore he could attract a large gathering of college students and other public figures. There he delivered a series of lectures. Rai Bahadur Shiv Dayal, a railway engineer, was so impressed by his lectures that he suggested to Bhakat Ishar Dass to start a big factory for Puran Singh.

Bhakat Ishar Dass was however well aware of the fact that in Japan he had embraced sanyas (asceticism) leaving his work in the lurch. So he advised Rai Bahadur Shiv Dayal to ask Puran Singh to first make the oil and the crystal before setting up a factory for him. Puran Singh agreed to this suggestion.

In Anarkali (Lahore) Bazaar, just at the back of the *Id gah*, there was a huge five-storeyed building with a wide and open courtyard. Bhakat Ishar Dass had shifted to his new bungalow, but this big house was still with him. They instructed Swamiji to set up a small unit in the countryard for extracting oil. Swamiji placed orders for big cauldrons with covers thereon and got them tinned. He got tubes fitted in those covers and made these interconnected to extract thymol.

In May he asked me to come to Lahore for looking after the guests. We used to go for a morning walk every day towards the river Ravi. One morning we heard a very loud but melodious chanting of 'Ala-hu' which prompted us to go in the direction from which it was coming. At a distance a young Mohammedan damsel was performing her prayer with her two hands raised towards the sky. (In those days there used to be a thick and big cluster of trees near the banks of Ravi.) That day we came back without disturbing her. Every morning our effort used to be to reach the bank of Ravi earlier than her, but we always failed. She was always there before us. Swamiji was under the impression, that she might be staying there even at night. So we thought of coming a bit late. When we reached there, the next day we did not hear that melodious voice. Immediately we noticed that she was coming with her prayer-mat rolled up. When she went away after finishing her prayers, we enquired about her from somebody and were told that she was a prostitute who had been ushered into the brothel very recently. She avoided staying there at night and spent her night here.

A lot-of people used to come during those days to meet Swamiji. In those days many Indians especially the young blood, were very much against the Britishers. Japan and Russia were fighting against each other. One boy was very anxious to go to Japan to fight for them. Since Swamiji had visited Japan, many young men came to meet him. One day a young man came and fell on Swamiji's feet and started weeping bitterly. Swamiji lifted him and embraced him and asked him what was the matter. But all he replied was 'Om.' He used to come often. One day he shared his inner agony with Swamiji. "I am a dead enemy of these bastard Britishers. I want to go to Japan and fight against these Englishmen. I believe in do or die. But I have no money to go to Japan." I had planned to go to Amritsar on that day. Swamiji instructed that boy (whom we now remember by the name of `Om') to go to the railway station and fetch from me the keys of my trunk. He took my keys from the railway station. Swamiji handed over to him the entire money and my ornaments. He left for Japan immediately.

When I returned from Amritsar, he informed me, "I have handed over your ornaments and money to Om." "I don't need all that, but you changed your programme only to pay off the loans and make adequate arrangements for your younger brothers", I reminded him.

When his mother came to know of the fact that he had handed over the money and the ornaments to someone, she rushed to Lahore on the first available train and without even wishing or greeting us, she straightaway demanded, "I learnt that Maya has handed over her ornaments and money to someone?" This enraged Puran Singh and he retorted, "Why do you accuse her? It was I who handed over the money and the ornaments." A severe altercation followed in which she accused him of trying to shield me. But soon everything was settled and mother and son were on the best of terms, even jesting with each other.

There were four cauldrons on different furnaces but the source of fire for all the four was the same. When thymol, aniseed oil, and citrus aurantium became ready, the whole of Anarkali Bazaar was engulfed in their scents. People passing through the bazaar flocked to our place.

Our place was a regular haunt for pious people. They did not find him depraved in any way but were in fact enamoured by his handsomeness, colour and power of concentration. In their opinion our's was an ideal life, where husband and wife though living in their worldly home considered themselves as *sanyasis* (ascetics). I left no room in looking after them.

We lived in that big house for three months — May, June and July. In those days Swamiji often discussed on spiritual knowledge and renunciation with me. Spiritual knowledge according to him helps us in testing the goodness in things and values. And for renunciation one should have the strength and will to abandon immediately the object for which one has developed even the slightest attachment. For relinquishment he prompted me to visualize the bad consequences which ultimately are to come out of the object for which I had some attraction. It helped me to repent thoroughly for having developed this weakness. In this way I developed a feeling of despondency. He also used to delineate those good aspects of Japanese life which had attracted him so and also such happenings as he had experienced in his personal life. Then he would explain to me their solemnity. He told me in minute details and devotion the purity and fearlessness of Japanese young damsels. I used to feel envious of them but accepted even their influence. The Japanese are crazy about flowers. They meet and watch flowers with all tenderness and respect. I could well visualize the beauty and the treatment towards flowers there. Like Panjabi *tappas* (couplets), in Japan there is a form of poetry known as *hoku*. Swamiji narrated to me an incident of an infant little girl who used to go to the well in the morning to fetch water for the family. One morning she noticed that beautiful flowers were embracing the parbuckle all around. She stood in silence and honour for the flowers as if she were in attendance to a very high dignitary. In a pensive mood, she wondered how and where to touch the parbuckle. Pitcher under the armpit, she kept on standing in solitude with her tender hand on her lips. Seeing her in this pensive mood and pose, someone, disturbing her tranquillity asked her, "What is the matter?" Struck by the human voice she spoke in verse:

> Flowers sitting with well-string
> How can I water bring?

From him I learnt that Japanese, leave alone speaking loudly in front of flowers do not even breathe hard. A Japanese, whoever he might be; while, paying a visit at another's house, would take a seat in the outer verandah (corridor) rather than knock or call out to anybody till someone happens to come out of the house. When he informs the master or mistress inside, he or she will immediately come out without any hitch or reservation. The Japanese do not worry others with their personal problems. They cannot dream of meeting any body in a dismayed or dejected mood and always appear with a smile. Like blossomed flowers they meet each other for a short while with all politeness and courtesy. Not very private people, yet they hate to exhibit their homes or household goods or woman and their ornaments and clothes considering it a wastage of time. In fact they value time so much that they do not waste time even discussing God or religion. As we cannot visualize the working of someone's mind while sitting with us, same is the case with their bodies. They sit still and do not give any indication of any kind with their hands, feet or eyes. So much so that they do not look straight at their king or priest. They keep very little household goods and do not worry about tables, chairs and cots. In fact, they love nature so much that they do not like to throw away even the fallen leaves in autumn even. Rather, they enjoy the falling of tree-leaves during autumn. But every Japanese house has a small pond in the courtyard where lotuses are grown. The Japanese readily accept students who go there for study as paying-guests. Their women look after their paying guests as their duty. The Japanese are well known for their hospitality. One student tried to hold the hand of the lady of the house when she went to give him his morning tea. The woman got her hand quietly freed and went away. Later on, the boy very much ashamed of his behaviour, wrote her a letter saying that he was deeply sorry for whatever had happened and that he was leaving.

The woman read the contents of the letter and handed over the same to her husband. She went to him and said, "I was very busy in the household work. In fact I ought to have come to you earlier. We are all travellers, travelling together in life. In this journey one slips at one moment and the other can slip at another occasion. Today you slipped and I came to your rescue. Tomorrow I may slip and at that time you may have to save me. Let us not fall together."

Swamiji wanted to convey to me the piousness and fearlessness of Japanese women. You cannot hope to transform anybody by punishing or defaming him. Forgiveness and love are the two weapons with which you can hope to mend others. That boy, afterwards turned out to be a very pious and intelligent gentleman. Swamiji's meaningful discourses left an ever lasting imprints on my mind.

Another incident he told me was about a sanyasi who had come to Japan. He could sit in meditation in the lap of the sea for hours together. This attracted many people, especially women and some even started worshipping him. Swamiji had accommodated that Sanyasi in his own room. But one night having noticed his sexual weakness he ordered him to vacate the room immediately. It was winter and outside the room it was very cold. In fact he had nowhere to go. Sardar Damodar Singh, who had come to Japan along with him also woke up and on hearing the whole episode requested Swamiji to allow him to stay on for the night. When people came to know of his hyprocrisy, he was castigated severally by one and all. Taking pity on him Swamiji paid for his fare back to India."

Another thing Swamiji hated was lustfullness in woman. He was not prepared to talk to any lustful woman, however educated she might be. But Swamiji was extremely kind at heart.

Once at Lahore, we found a woman along with her ailing son, pustules spreading all over his body, sitting on the roadside. Her son was crying with pain. The woman, weeping bitterly looked towards us for help. Swamiji immediately took the ailing boy in his arms and got him admitted to an hospital and arranged a room for him. He used to visit the hospital everyday to enquire about his health. When the boy recovered completely, he handed over him to his mother and paid for all the hospital charges. Somebody pointed out that where was the need to spend so much money when he could be easily admitted in a Government hospital free of cost.

Lamenting his mean attitude Swamiji, said "There were no limitations in the beginning of the universe. Maya, just pity this man and his mean thinking. We are not worried about our future. Money, kept unused for a long time stagnates. In Europe there lived a man with a very liberal attitude and deep vision. One day he noticed the horrible plight of chimney-labourers. Their sparkling eyes left a lasting impression on his heart. He thought, it is because of these chimney labourers that our big industries were flourishing. They must be honoured by arranging sumptuous dinners for them in big hotels. He started spending his money by inviting them for dinners at luxurious hotels where they were normally not allowed to enter. In this way he spent his entire money. He thought his money had exhausted because it was a stale one. Now I should raise fresh funds for this good cause. For collecting money, he used to visit rich lords, extending his hat as his begging-bowl. Every rich lord knew this generous man very well. He would not accept from them less than a pound (£). Later on, he used to take these children of black labourers out for dinner to good hotels. Whatever money was left, he would throw it in river Thames, thinking that it would become stale-money tomorrow. By narrating such episodes, he made me generous and liberal. I never doubted whatever he told me.

Our house was open to all needy people for their daily needs. Whatever they demanded, they were provided with. Many rich people who wanted their money to be used for propitious purposes would pour it into Swamiji's pockets or would secretly leave it under his pillow.

It was summer and we often used to order cold drinks, ice and fruits for our guests. The shopkeepers warned Bhakat Ishar Dass who was Swamiji's business partner, that he would have to bear a big loss from this business, as money was being squandered away. But no one dared to say anything to Swamiji. Bhakat Ishar Dass too respected Swamiji greatly. Three months passed away in this manner in extracting oils, giving religious discourses and entertaining needy people. Eventually two pounds of thymol crystal, two pounds of aniseed oil, and some ounces of citrus aurantium were ready. With feeling of great jubilation Swamiji filled some samples of these oils in different bottles and took them to show to Bhakat Ishar Dass. When he reached there he met with a large assembly of people who had gathered to discuss something. Swamiji was feeling over-jubilant at his success. Swamiji passed around these oils to everybody present there, and was appreciated by one and all. Swamiji was over-anxious and over-enthusiastic about his success and was sure that all of them would immediately volunteer to invest enough money for installing a big factory. But instead, they advised Swamiji to continue with the preparation of these oils. They suggested that these samples be sent to the market to ascertain their market value first.

The moment this was said, Swamiji exploded, "You all are crooked people." After uttering these words, he rushed back home and I don't know from where he gathered the super-human strength to smash all the furnaces and to throw away all the cauldrons on the ground. I was an eye witness to all this, standing near the window on the first floor. Only a painter could portray the majesty, the shining features and the furiosity of his face at that moment. To me he seemed impersonating Lord Siva who had smashed the whole yaga (religious ceremony) celebrations and sacrificial vessels of Prajapati Daksha, where Parvati (sati) had to sacrifice herself.

After smashing everything, he came to the first floor and threw away all the money that was left unspent for this project (in those days mostly silver coins were used). He sent a message to Bhakat Ishar Dass to come and take charge of his property. He left everything there with all the doors open. This was the first occasion when I fully felt the feeling of renunciation. Nothing could deviate him from his firm determination. He gave an ample proof of what he had been singing all his life:

> Even for name sake, do not leave in this world any token.
> Neither your body nor your mind or life here.
> Don't consider any place as your residence in this perishable world,
> Remain homeless in a home and placeless in a place.
> What help can this expectant world render to you?
> Don't hope any real help from them in this world or the next one to come.

From there we immediately proceeded for Dehradun. Sometime back we had received a letter from one Mrs. Wellman of America, a disciple of Swami Ram Tirath. She had expressed a desire to Swamiji to accompany her to Teehri to meet Swami Ram Tirath in the third week of July. He left a message for her saying that we were leaving for Dehradun and she was free to come to Dehradun and stay at the Railway rest house and that we would make arrangements with the orderly to convey to us the news of her arrival at Dehradun where we would be putting up with Joti Sarup, also a disciple of Swami Ram Tirath.

All disciples of Swami Ram Tirath respected Swamiji greatly. As Swami Ram Tirath considered him his co-incarnate.

Singing and weeping under the spell of spiritual intoxication, he hired a tonga. When the tonga driver asked for the destination, he burst at him in anger, "you are not even aware of my destination? Take me to hell."

"I don't know the way to hell", the tonga driver innocently replied. By this time Swamiji curbed his anger and very soon got fully recovered. He instructed the tonga driver to proceed to the railway station.

Very soon we were heading for Dehradun. It had been very hot in Lahore. But next morning when we had crossed Laksar, romantic and soothing sights of thick forests and the flowing Ganges met our eyes. Tranquillity, we felt, is indescribable. As we advanced towards our destination we were fortunate in enjoying many water-falls on the way. The cool breeze endeared us in abundance. The picturesque scenes and their soothing effect, enchanted Swami Puran so much that he began singing:

> The morning breeze is the messenger of my beloved,
> How can I have a wink of sleep
> when arrows from my darlings' eyes
> Are about to hurt me?
> Why do you forcibly snatch my heart?
> Am I, otherwise, reluctant to hand over?

Seeing him singing and intoxicated with joy, I was drawn to him further. All the songs sung by him still echo in my mind and whenever I recall them, they come back easily to me. He was an artist and the overflow of his sentiments and feelings of his joy, streamed through his songs. Even his essays speak of his intoxicated spirit.

When we reached Dehradun next morning it was drizzling. We proceeded to the residence of Joti Sarup in a tonga. As we passed by the houses on the way we found them neat and decorated, cleansed by the rain water. The sweet melodious voice oozing out of the clouds seemed to welcome us. Whenever I recall that experience I still feel rejoiced and overwhelmed with pleasure. The romantic and soothing scenery of this valley, prompted me to desire to settle down at Dehradun for ever. The fulfilment of my earnest desire was soon realised when we permanently shifted to Dehradun in 1904. Meanwhile, Mrs. Wellman had also reached Dehradun and we all left for Mussorie. Swamiji made me agree to stay at somebody's house at Mussorie. He said, "All these are my own homes." Though totally unknown, yet they agreed to keep me with them. Two and a half months of my stay with Swami Puran Singh had made me to fully believe the prevalence of the same spirit in all people. It is within our power to realize and kindle the love fire in their hearts. Just as hidden fire does not kindle unless it is blown with air, similarly if you have sincere love for others, all will love you in return with the same intensity and devotion.

Swamiji left for Teehri along with Mrs. Wellman. On reaching there they found that Swami Ram Tirath had left for Kedarnath. From Kedarnath they were told that he had left for Badri Narain. The Raja of Teehri had provided one palanquin for Mrs. Wellman, but Swamiji preferred to walk the whole intricate hilly way on foot and got serious injuries on his feet.

The house where I was staying belonged to a big and prosperous family. All of them had great regards for me. They had two daughters, two daughters-in-law, two sons and four children. The landlady was very nice to me. I tried to help them in their domestic chores. Nobody in the family seemed unknown or alien to me.

Swamiji returned from Teehri after two months. Mrs. Wellman, went back to America having enjoyed the spiritual sermons of Swami Ram Tirath and we returned to Lahore.

On coming back in October 1904 along with my mother-in-law, father-in-law and two brothers-in-law Wazir Singh and Ram Singh, we hired the third floor of a house and settled down there along with Swamiji's parents and brothers. People at Lahore still had great respect for Swamiji. They held only Bhakat Ishar Dass as guilty. It was not long before people started inviting him for lectures. He could deliver lectures on any subject and with such gusto and conviction, that people loved listening to him. In the course of one of these lectures it was suggested to him to manufacture articles of domestic use. He started his work in that very house. He whitened mustard oil and that too without odour. He also manufactured boot polish and wax. All these experiments went on until December 1904. He would polish the boots of persons who visited us. When he was fully satisfied with the quality of his boot polish, he trained a young man with the know-how and helped him in starting his business. I left for my parents at Rawalpindi in December 1904.

We often had meetings against the Britishers at our house. Ramakant Roy - the anarchist from Bengal — who was Swamiji's classmate in Japan also visited us. Our landlord who was a public prosecuter with the government did not like the going on in our house, but he did not dare to say anything to Swamiji for very long. One day, however, he gathered enough courage to entreat to Swamiji to vacate his house saying that his daughter and son-in-law would be coming to Lahore, and that he would need this floor for them. I was at Rawalpindi at that time. Swamiji hired a house in Sooter market and shifted to that place.

During this time four students of Medical College, Lahore were expelled for carrying out anti-government propaganda. All the students requested the Principal to revise his decision. Even some respectable persons approached the Principal to pardon those students as the annual examinations were at hand. But the Principal did not agree to their suggestion. The students decided to smash the entire college property next morning. They came to the college premises quite early in the morning. They broke all window-panes, chairs, tables and laboratory equipment. The Principal called the police but the students had left the place much in advance. The police could not arrest any one.

When Swamiji came to know of it, he along with his other friends persuaded the students to assemble at the temple of

Bhadar Kali. It was a big temple with a very wide courtyard. He exhorted them to go on a strike unless and until the Principal agreed to revoke his decision. In the gathering there were some students who had pro-government views and some were weak-hearted. So it was decided that all of them be kept on constant watch and vigil. All the exits were blocked so that no student could go out. There was rejoicing all over the place and preparations for their meals started. All of them were provided with *karah* (pudding of flour, sugar and butter) along with *puris* (thin fried cakes), sweetmeats and their favourite dishes. Swamiji delivered lectures to those students day and night. Their professors were not allowed to enter the premises. In this way all the students remained under control for some days. Ultimately the Principal was compelled to accede to their demands. All the students started attending their classes regularly. The total expenses were borne more by others and less by Swamiji. He enjoyed spending money as if he were playing the game of rupee-colours. He sang in pleasure:-

> I am sprinkling colours in abundance,
> On the variegated people of this world,
> The game of colours is in full swing,
> And I have drenched them through and through.

In this way he collected immense money but never spent a paisa for himself or his household expenses.

At Lahore he revived the monthly paper *Thundering Dawn*, started by him in Japan. People were so much impressed with its first issue that they immediately sent their subscriptions for two years.

It was in Lahore that he met Rai Sahib Bishan Dass, who seeing his talent go wasted on boot-polish (for exhibiting his art and genius Swamiji had once polished his shoes as well), appointed him the Principal of Victoria Diamond Jubilee Technical Institute, Lahore at a monthly salary of Rs.120/-. Side by side he went on editing his monthly paper.

He had been doing all these works from December 1904 to March 1905. On March 5, 1905 we were blessed with a daughter. So Swamiji along with my mother-in-law came down to Rawalpindi to see me. At that time there was an old lady working for me. While sitting in my room, Swamiji put his hand in his pocket to take out a paper on which he had written an essay and which he wanted to read out to me. While he was taking out that paper a paisa fell on the ground. The maid servant picked up the coin and returned it to Swamiji. But Swamiji refused, saying, "You keep it with you". Hearing this, she felt so rejoiced that the pleasure, out of her gratitude, started radiating from her face. Swamiji was so touched by her poverty and pleasure that he instantly took out all his money and gave it to her. But she was hesitant to accept it. Swamiji entreated, "In your previous birth you had deposited this amount with me and I am returning you your own money." His mother was overhearing all this and came into the room. Scolding him, she said, "Oh my foolish son, why don't you give this money to me instead?" Her son, who was enjoying complete peace and pleasure of a higher and elevated world got angry with his mother. "In spite of the fact that you are my mother, you stoop so low and talk so mean?" For a while they remained quarrelling. Their clash thundered and sparked as if positive and negative wires of electricity had come into contact. When both became quiet and normal, the son said, "Dear Mam, will you like to take *pooras* (sweet round cakes) from Ganesh confectioner's shop?" The mother smiled and nodded in affirmative. The mother and son enjoyed those *pooras* up to their fill and also offered some to the old maid servant. We named our daughter Gargi.

In the district of Kangra there are many temples. There are numerous stories and miracles associated with these temples such as the sparkling of fire and flow from hot water springs. At a little distance from volcano there is a hot water spring known as Mani Karan. Here people put rice tied in a small cloth and throw the same in that spring. After sometime they come up on the surface as fried *pooris* (thin fried cakes) come out of boiling oil. In my childhood I had visited the place and had witnessed the same with my own eyes.

In March 1905, with the bursting of volcano, a severe earthquake shook the whole of India. The entire temple was shattered to pieces. The impact of this earthquake was felt even in Peshawar, Rawalpindi and Calcutta. Cracks appeared in many buildings. In many cities houses came down. In Jwalamukhi temple there was a huge gold deposit of maunds. The government instructed the police to guard the debris in the temple.

Certain influential people in Lahore decided to send a delegation to Bhagsu Nath for recovering the gold. Dr. Sunder Dass was requested to lead this delegation. He requested Swamiji to accompany him. About twenty qualified people left for Jwalamukhi. They were able to recover about two and a half maunds of gold from the debris.

Later some committees were constituted for the re-construction of the temple, but Swamiji did not participate in any of these Committees.

I came to Lahore in April 1905. Once, at a gathering of musicians at Badami Bagh, Vishnu Digambar was also invited. He surpassed everybody taking his *alap* to such musical heights that it appeared as though clouds were thundering. Then he dropped his *alap* to mute speech and there was pin-drop silence. Swamiji was enamoured by his musical excellence. I was also present in that gathering. Swamiji was very keen that I should adopt Vishnu Digamber as my music guru. Vishnu Digamber started a music school under the name of "Sangeet Bhawan" in the outskirts of Lahore. People joined that institution for learning music.

Although there were other teachers for the junior classes, Swamiji was keen that I should learn music only from Vishnu Digamber and he requested Vishnu Digamber for the same, but was told that he could spare time early in the morning only. Swamiji used to take me to Sangeet Bhawan, which was at a distance of two and a half miles, at five every morning. He accompanied me for a few days, but afterwards he said to me, "Now you are fully known to the way to Sangeet Bhawan and can go alone."

Since the music books were in Hindi, I gradually picked up that language.

Vishnu Digamber tested my voice for a day or two. After that he said, "If you keep on learning music from me, you will be able to sing, if not better, at least of my quality." But unfortunately I could not continue for more than six months. I still remember the *ragas* and *gamuts* taught by him.

In June 1905 Mitra, a Bengali post-graduate student of Government College Lahore, contracted typhoid. He was putting up in the hostel. Swamiji brought him to our home and entrusted me the job of looking after him. Being a typhoid patient, doctors instructed him not to move from his bed. So I had to give him bedpan, sponge him and keep cool coarse cloth on his forehead from time to time or do other jobs. How could my mother-in-law digest all this? She did not allow me to enter the kitchen. She even used to taunt or scold me, so that I might stop doing service to the patient, under provocation. Fearing that the mother and her son might quarrel over this issue, I never mentioned her taunts to Swamiji.

Hardial and Khudadad, two other students visited us often for enquiring about his health. When they saw how well he was looked after they were very happy. All of them belonged to the revolutionary party.

After some years Hardial M.A. was externed from the country. There was no case against Khudadad and he got a job in Engineering College, Roorke. He generally visited us at Lahore. In November 1905 Khudadad came to know that a big industrial fair was being held at Banaras. He persuaded Swamiji to participate and deliver lectures there. At that time Swamiji had no boots, trousers, coat or a hat. He said, "My friend, you are asking me to go to Banaras, but I have nothing to wear". Hearing this Khudadad handed over his suit and boots to him. The boots fitted perfectly but the trousers had to be restitched to suit his size. Swamiji went to Banaras donning these clothes. Khudadad was so much devoted to Swamiji that he could do anything for him. Their friendship was exemplary.

At Banaras Swamiji delivered a series of lectures on certain scientific topics which were enormously appreciated by the people. But on coming back to Lahore, he forgot all about his lectures at Banaras and got busy in his routine work.

Doctor Iqbal had deep love and high regards for Swamiji. Whenever he came to our house, he recited his poetry with ardent passion. He had a great dislike for religious preachers. One day he recited:

Theologians have enough arguments to scandalize wine,
But Iqbal is stubborn enough to yield to their game.

Swamiji had a good habit of appreciating works of other writers, and would invariably find good points in every writing. At Lahore, the days passed on like this. Swamiji would offer his shoes to the person going bear-footed in the scorching sun or his blanket to a person trembling with biting cold. One day he returned home bare-headed. My mother-in-law got furious with him because she considered it inauspicious.

"No dear mother, Ravi river was shivering in cold, I offered her my turban."

Though I always felt happy about his generosity my mother-in-law never reconciled to appreciate his gestures.

In November 1905 we received a letter from Swami Narain that Swami Ram Tirath was visiting Haridwar and would be staying at the residence of Lala Joti Sarup. All the followers of Swami Ram Tirath had been informed accordingly. Many of his followers rushed to Haridwar to catch a glimpse of him. When Swami Ram Tirath's wife whom he had left came to know that Swami Ram Tirath was staying at Haridwar she along with her two sons and daughter reached there.

Swamiji informed Swami Ram Tirath that his wife, along with Madan, Brahmanand and Jasodra had come to see him.

Swami Ram Tirath was shocked to know that his family members had come to meet him. He entreated Swami Puran to somehow convince her to go back.

Swami Puran got enraged at his strange behaviour and said, "No, this can't be. Why do you discriminate against them? Other people are coming to meet you. Aren't they human beings? I will not allow this thing to happen. You must meet them."

Swami Ram Tirath replied, "Since you insist, they can meet me for five minutes."

His wife, clad in dirty, unwashed clothes and trembling badly entered his room along with her children and bowed down to touch his feet. But Swami Ram Tirath moved aside to avoid her touch.

Swami Puran was shocked to see his behaviour and said, "Swamiji, you do not believe in untouchability and discrimination. What is this?"

Swami Puran then asked Brahmanand, his younger son, to read out his lesson to Swami Ram Tirath.

The boy started the reading of his book, but Swami Ram Tirath kept his eyes closed and did not utter a single word. Swami Puran requested him, "Swamiji kindly bless him." But Swami Ram Tirath remained unmoved. Then Swami Puran placed before him a basket full of grapes and requested Swami Ram Tirath to hand over the same to Brahmanand.

Swami Ram Tirath replied, "You may hand it over to him. Their meeting time is over. Kindly get them their tickets so that they could go back to their place."

Money was no problem in those days. Many rich followers were in attendance at that time. They authorised Swami Puran to give them as much money as he wished to. Swami Puran sent them back with enough money and their railway tickets.

When Swami Puran narrated to me the whole incident, I was so moved that I started crying and entreated Swami Puran to take me to her. "Unless and until I meet the family members of Swami Ram Tirath, I cannot feel at rest. Emotions have swept me very severely. Let us go to Murariwala. We will not only have the pleasure of seeing Swamiji's birth place but will also have a chance to meet and talk to his family members.

Seeing me shattered and shaken, Swamiji agreed to my proposal. Next day we left for Murariwala. After passing through many narrow lanes we reached Swami Ram Tirath's house which was constructed on a high plinth. The moment they heard the happy news of our visit, the whole family rushed to receive us. Swami Ram Tirath's old father, blessed us with his trembling hands. I embraced his wife tightly and wept bitterly. She also started weeping. We had brought with us fruits, sweets and clothes for them. The children's faces radiated with pleasure and blossomed on seeing these gifts. Then we visited those lanes where Swami Ram Tirath had played in his childhood and the school where he had received his early education. But my heart remained shattered and shaken as before.

Khudadad and Hardial had also come to Haridwar to meet Swami Ram Tirath. Khudadad composed a poem about Swami Ram Tirath's smile and its impact on the on - lookers. It was a Persian couplet which denoted that "when I had the privilege and pleasure of witnessing the full-smiled face of Swami Ram Tirath, all the secrets of life flashed at my inward eye."

Swami Ram Tirath declared in the presence of all that Swami Puran was his co-incarnation. He asked Joti Sarup, "Do help Puran. The government will not do anything for him. Please see that his training and knowledge do not go waste."

Joti Sarup replied, "I have hundreds of bigha land at Dohiwala with a pucca constructed bungalow. He can use it in any way he likes and I am prepared to invest as much money as he desires."

Swami Ram Tirath and Swami Narain later on left for Teehri and others who had assembled there left for their respective places after getting a message of fighting for the freedom of the country. We also returned to Lahore.

The followers of Swami Ram Tirath started assembling in our house at Sootar Mandi. They were very much impressed by Swami Puran's renunciation and had full faith in the assertion that he was Swami Ram Tirath's co-incarnation. *Sanyasis* were given due respect at our place.

One day a hefty self-appointed guru came to our house. Swami Puran was at that time sitting amidst his family members and enjoying their company. My father-in-law, mother-in-law, two brothers, one sister, his mother's sister, and Gargi, were all around him. They were happy for the fact that they had been blessed with a daughter-in-law as well as a grand-daughter. Seeing Swami Puran, fully engrossed with his family-members, he taunted, "What type of a monk are you? I was told that you were a real *sanyasi* though living with your family-members."

Swamiji got enraged and retorted in the same strain, "Oh complete slave of these coloured clothes, are you aware of the flight of those sparrows, who flutter in the dust and fight amongst themselves. When they think of their flight, they immediately fly to the sky brushing and removing the dust on their wings and start swimming in the air."

There was no hypocrisy in the life of Swamiji. Whenever he heard or saw anything objectionable, he would immediately burst on the person like a thundering of the sky. He had no ill-will for anybody. He would not hurt anybody knowingly or consciously. He would scold any person who spoke or smiled sarcastically. Those sitting hear him would be surprised to hear the fierce scolding to the guilty in comparison to his guilt. But immediately he would become normal as if nothing had happened.

My mother-in-law narrated to me an incident of his childhood, when he was in the fifth class. A piece of paper on which he was writing flew away. He asked his sister to bring that paper. She retorted, "Wait a bit". He became so enraged that he beat her up severely and himself picked up the paper.

When the mother arrived, Ganga started weeping and complained against his beating. The mother always had a soft corner for her daughters as compared to her sons. She became angry with her son, "Why did you beat your sister?"

The son replied, "Mother, first listen to the whole incident. My paper, on which I was writing flew far away. I asked her to bring that paper, but she never cared to obey me. I myself picked up my paper and gave her a mild slap".

The sister retorted, "But I agreed to bring the paper".

Her son shot back, "Just see mother, she is telling a lie. She said, "Wait a bit," meaning thereby that she was not prepared to bring the paper immediately."

Even in his childhood he would not listen to anybody and would consider himself always correct. My mother-in-law narrated another incident when he was in the fourth class. One morning he picked up his satchel and said, "Something is missing in it." His elder sister Lajan checked up all his books and exercise books and found it complete. He again picked up his satchel and complained, "I say something is missing". His sister became furious and checked them again and found that somebody had torn out some paper out of his exercise book. Seeing this he said, "Wasn't I right?"

Similarly he was able to detect a lie. When I once asked him, how he did it he said, "As you are able to distinguish between the resounding sound of a filled and unfilled pitcher, similarly I am able to detect immediately an artificial, untrue and sycophant person."

Everybody was realizing that Swami Puran had not been provided with a job he was fit for. But even then people did provide him with some assignment. There was a glass-factory at Ambala. Its owners wanted to manufacture chrome-oxide in green colour which was not manufactured in India.

Swamiji agreed to manufacture it for them provided they advanced him rupees five hundred for the raw-material. The factory-owner immediately remitted him the desired amount. He immediately purchased sulphur and red moss. He made a furnace at the roof of the top floor of our house at Sootar Mandi. Within fifteen days chrome-oxide was ready and was sent to the factory-owner at Ambala. The factory owner remitted to him another sum of rupees seven hundred. In this way he was able to earn the amount we needed for our daily use.

I had been learning music from Vishnu Digambar for the last one year. I had learnt first four books of music. In October 1906 we received a letter from Joti Sarup saying, "If you have not started any other work, kindly come to Dehradun so that we may chalk out some plan."

He went to the school authorities with that letter and requested them to accept his resignation as he was planning to go to Dehradun. He asked me to keep the luggage ready so that we could leave for Dehradun immediately. We would call our father and mother afterwards. He wired to Joti Sarup that we were coming. His carriage was there at the railway station to receive us when we reached Dehradun.

Joti Sarup was to lay the foundation stone of Mahadevi Kanya Mahavidyala, named after his wife. Joti Sarup happily announced to his wife, "Swami Puran, who is in fact Ram's co-incarnate, has come to Dehradun for laying the foundation stone of your school."

I was employed at rupees fifty per month as a music teacher for the junior classes in the same school. I used to teach the students, playing at the harmonium daily for two hours. After some days Joti Sarup convened a meeting in which besides him, some prominent personalities like Baldev Singh, Seth Lachhmi Chand participated. Everybody recommended the manufacturing of washing soap, which was needed by rich and poor alike. Swamiji desired that raw-material for at least one thousand maunds be ordered.

Orders for big cauldrons were placed with the iron-smiths. Orders were also placed for soap-cutting machines, trolleys, oil and caustic soda. He wrote a letter to the minister of Teehri State, who sent an order for five hundred maunds of soap for his state. Five feet high furnaces were got prepared on which the big cauldrons were to be placed. For the revolving of trolleys, slanting roads were chalked out. When the entire raw-material was received, we shifted to Dohiwala where Joti Sarup had enough land and a house to live in.

3. Dohiwala

In those days Dohiwala was a thick forest. It was surrounded by huge and tall trees of Saal and Sandal. These trees were so thick and sprawling that the rays of the sun could not pass through them. The twigs of jasmine plants and those of rose embracing the trunks of the trees and climbing upwards spread fragrance all over the area. The green grass had grown all over the earth. The river Soung flowed from there. Swamiji was enchanted when he saw these thick forests of Dohiwala. He used to take me out to the forest, embrace the tree trunks and dance with intense pleasure.

We felt as if every leaf of the trees was ripened with love-sentiments. I was also fully thrilled with joy. He used to roam about the forest and sing aloud in rejoicing the natural atmosphere.

> Oh sweetheart fill in my measure with something
> That your tipsy may feel fully absolved of this
> and the other world.

He was so much in tune with every object of nature that he felt as if he were hearing the throbbings of his own heart in it. He did not find any difference in his own throbbings and that of a grass straw lying on the dust.

The station master of Dohiwala was also a self-seeker. One morning he, forced and inspired by his inner spiritual inkling, went out in the forest in search of a godly-power. At a distance he saw an embodiment of a dazzling spiritual beauty, tears dripping from his eyes. Dazzled with such an abnormal and enchanting sight, he fell on his feet. Swamiji held him and embraced him in sheer joy and pleasure. Dazed and dazzled completely, the station master could not utter a single word. In this way many people felt spiritual peace and pleasure by his sheer touch.

A saint visited the house of the station master off and on. One day the station master brought him to our place. At that time Swamiji, absorbed in himself, was singing loudly:

> I find you everywhere, all over,
> Not that I yearn to have a glimpse of you,

> Not that I am in quest of you,
> Oh dazzling power, your beauty is stunning,
> And I feel your presence in every moment of my life.

When the saint saw him singing in intoxication unaware of anything, he was stunned. He realized that though he had the privilege of meeting so many saints, he was yet to see anyone in this strange spiritual state of mind.

Swamiji opened his eyes and the station master bowed on his feet. I was also standing there.

The saint remained standing there in bewilderment. He enquired, "Which mortification do you practice?"

He retorted, "Oh enslaved *Sanyasi* (ascetic), what do you mean by mortification? A king's son is a king even at the time of his birth. I am sitting in His cradle and enjoying. He is in me and I am in Him".

He always kept me in his company. He used to read out to me his every writing and ask my opinion. In this way he always tried to infuse in me all types of his knowledge. Maddened with intrinsic emotions, the poet Puran never needed anything. Sentiments and emotions flooded in him. Within a second he could go beyond the horizon. The sky was the limit. I always did whatever he asked me to do.

. While getting the factory work from the labourers — men and women — he would, at times, ask them to go and rest. No body would mind any of his gestures.

One day he accompanied a newly wedded bride to the railway station to entrain her. The bridegroom was also standing by and all her relatives were weeping. Standing by her palanquin, he started weeping bitterly and sang:

> When the bride bids goodbye to her native place,
> Small hair on the body stands still and the throat dries up.

He went on singing this couplet the whole day. To none, any of his gestures looked extraordinary.

Even a very small thing could inspire his mind to fly to the farthest heights. He had never developed any sense of duality in his mind and he had the power to remove anybody's misgivings or misunderstandings in a second. People were prepared to do any sacrifice for him but he did not accept anything from anybody. Whatever people offered to him, he would distribute it then and there amongst the people present there.

Having witnessed so many happenings of this nature, no material thing had any value for me. Neither I needed anything nor I ever thought of saving anything for future. He did not allow me to keep anything under lock and key. With a feeling of anger he used to say, "You suspect others to be thieves and use locks. The thief lives in you. Unless you have an inkling of this feeling, you will never think of a thief." This preaching of his has left such an indelible impact on my mind that I never keep anything under lock and key till today.

Although people were not residing at Dohiwala in those days and the residents had not witnessed free and open love, yet people were not surprised at any of Swamiji's gestures. He used to embrace every one – be a man, girl, tree or animal. People felt happy over this. Those unlettered residents were wonder-struck over the behaviour of this highly educated man. He had a charming and extra-ordinary personality. Whenever he embraced a cow or a bull and rubbed his face with their faces, the animals had never misbehaved with him, rather they raised their necks for a gentle itching. This novel behaviour of his had become known all over the area and people flocked to our place to see and meet him.

He could not keep anybody's secret to himself. Whenever somebody started narrating his story to him, he would entreat to him, "Brother, do not narrate to me anything which I cannot pass on to others." So people did not divulge anything to him which they would like to keep as secret. He never discriminated with anybody.

It was rainy season and thick clouds had covered whole of the sky. The ground was all green. He was so much impressed and inspired by this natural and beautiful scene that he went out to the forest singing the following couplet by Nazir:

> The flush greenery on the ground
> The thick blackening of the sky,
> Who else can portray and paint
> This excellent and unique scene of God.

He had become one with God. He saw a lean man riding on a black horse. The horse was healthy, strong and attractive.

When that man came near him he shouted at him, "Stop and get down." It was a completely deserted place. Terrified by his sudden shout, he descended from the horseback. He snatched the horse from that man and with a jump rode on him. He disappeared in a second and the poor terrified owner looked on helplessly. The owner thought of approaching the station master and describing his height, face features and appearance to him. He complained of the snatching of his horse. The station master pacified him, "He is a holy person, you are fortunate that he has selected your horse for a ride." He came to our bungalow riding the horse. I was wonder-struck to see him controlling such an agile horse, which was not prepared to stand still for a second. In a spur of moment, he took the horse to the railway station. When he was approaching the railway station, the station master happily said, "look, the Sun god is riding your horse and coming towards us."

Four months passed by in the manufacturing of soap. Four hundred maunds of soap were despatched to Teehri state. The remaining soap was in the process of manufacturing. During these four months he enriched me with a great deal of knowledge by illustrating many points from daily and practical life. He got 'Yoga Vasishta' from Bombay especially for me. He used to read it out to me. He neither talked anything irrelevent nor would he allow anybody to do so. We never discussed any commercial problems amongst ourselves.

Men with revolutionary views visited us off and on and intimated us the wrong doings of the Britishers. Somebody gave us the information that injustice was done to Khudadad at Roorki. One evening some Englishmen were busy with a game of golf. Accidently the ball struck at the boots of Khudadad and was obstructed. One Englishman who was very much enraged, abused Khudadad by saying, "Damn fool". Hearing this abuse, Khudadad demanded apology from him. Instead of apologizing, he again said, "Damn fool." Khudadad took out his watch from his pocket and declared, "I will wait for five minutes for your apology. If you do not apologize within this time, I will shower on you unheard absurd and filthy abuses in Panjabi." And after five minutes when the Englishman did not apologize, he gave him a bundle of abuses with translations into English. As a result Khudadad was dismissed from service.

On hearing this Swamiji got very angry. He sent a telegram to Khudadad asking him to come to Dohiwala immediately.

The chemist-in-charge of the Forest Research Institute at Dehradun had gone abroad for his advanced studies. This vacancy was to be filled up. The selection committee decided to appoint Puran Singh in his place. This was the result of his lectures he had delivered at Banaras. A letter was received at Dohiwala requesting him to come to Dehradun and take charge of this office. Swamiji contacted Joti Sarup to know his reaction.

But Joti Sarup was worried about the material scattered all around.

At Kuhenwale, a minister of Teehri State owned some land and a bungalow. He had standing orders from the Raja of Teehri to help Swami Puran whenever the need arose. Swami Puran asked Joti Sarup to accompany him to the Minister of Teehri for advice. They went to Kuhenwale and acquainted him with the situation. He said, "There is nothing to worry. You pay Joti Sarup the total amount so far spent and bring the entire material to Kuhenwale."

He asked his mother and other family members to come to Kuhenwale. The day we were to leave for Kuhenwale with our personal luggage and board the train, we saw Khudadad detraining at Dohiwala with his luggage. Swamiji advised him to keep sitting in the train.

We all reach Kuhenwale. Swamiji left for Dehradun the next morning to take charge of his post. He brought Joti Sarup to Kuhenwale along with him and settled the entire accounts with the minister of Teehri state. The minister paid the entire amount to Joti Sarup and got all the material at Dohiwala shifted to Kuhenwale.

For some time the factory-work went on at Kuhenwale, but it was realized that it could not prosper here. One engineer offered to pay five thousand rupees for the entire material. The engineer paid rupees five hundred in cash and the balance in the form of a draft. Myself and Khudadad were sitting beside them.

At the time of handing over the cash to Swami Puran, the engineer uttered something which was not audible to us. But this enraged Swami Puran and he flung the bag full of money at the engineer which struck at his chest. The engineer started vomitting but was saved in time. The engineer apologized to Swami Puran for his sarcastic remarks. The poor fellow had to bear physical punishment, apologize and pay money. The engineer took the entire material and went away.

We stayed in Dehradun from 1906 to 1913 in the bungalow just behind the general post-office. In August 1906 a group of followers of Swami Ram Tirath visited Dehradun, and Swami Puran accompanied them to Badrinarain for meeting Swami Ram Tirath. But Swamiji had already left for Budhekidar.

The way to Budhekidar is very intricate and baffling. One had to tread over a log ten feet long and only nine inches wide. About hundred feet beneath the water of Gangotri flowed. All of them were able to cross that log. When they met Swami Ram Tirath, he said, "I have deputed Swami Puran to you on my behalf. Why do you come here and disturb me?" Then Ram Tirath took all of them to Gangotri. The way to Gangotri was so intricate and baffling that all other followers, except Sami Puran, returned in disgust. Swami Ram Tirath after reaching Gangotri expressed his desire, "how nice it will be if you, along with your wife, shift to this place. On the top of one mountain, I will stay and on the other opposite top, you both can stay." Swami Puran returned to Dehradun after some days. He narrated all the incidents to us, including the wish of Swami Ram Tirath. This proposal appealed to me but my mother-in-law got very angry. Then we heard the news that on October 18, 1906 (Diwali day) Swami Ram Tirath went into the Ganges and never came out. Three days had passed. The Raja of the state got many nets thrown in the river and even divers had tried their best. But they could not detect his body. This demise shocked Swami Puran very much and he was completely shattered. Without taking anything with him he immediately left for Teehri. Hundreds of people had assembled at Teehri. Swami Narain was also there. The clothes of Swami Ram Tirath were still lying at the banks of Ganga waiting for their wearer.

Swami Puran went to different corners of the river and called him aloud, "Oh Swamiji, if your corpse does not come out of the water and float, Puran will jump for death from this very place."

There was a big gathering including high officials of the Raja and other visitors. Everybody was terrified. Swami Narain caught hold of Swami Puran tightly and entreated, "Oh my master, please don't do that".

All assembled there were chanting "Om" again and again. Very soon Swami Ram Tirath's corpse floated up. Even after four days there was no sign of damage on the dead body except that it was swollen. Observing the *sanyasi* rites, his corpse was submerged in the holy waters of Ganga.

Swami Puran returned to Dehradun, but with heavy heart. At night he used to look at the stars and weep bitterly for reunion with his master.

In August 1907, we were blessed with a son. Swami Narain christened him Narain. Later he was known as Madanmohan Singh, but his nickname remained Narain.

During the monsoons ascetics from Rishikesh and Haridwar visited Badri Nairan. On their way, a majority of them stayed with us.

Once four learned ascetics were staying with us. They had long conversations with Swami Puran and benefited much from him so much so that they were reluctant to leave our place. Swami Puran's grandfather whom we called Bapuji, did not like their staying at our house fearing that his grandson might again become an ascetic. When Swami Puran was away to Forest Research Institute for his duty, Bapuji used to have long discussions with those *sanyasis*. I was always under this constant fear that they might take offence and leave our place.

One day I disclosed my apprehension to Swamiji, "Bapuji keeps on discussing with these *sanyasis* and I apprehend that they may leave our place under provocation."

Swamiji replied, "we have no ill-will for those sanyasis. If they leave our place under provocation you need not worry about it. I have become fearless."

Bapuji did not spare them. He told them, "a sanyasi should not stay more than a night in the house of a married worldly man." Hearing these words the three sanyasis left our place. Brahmanand who was a graduate, did not accompany them. Those three had left our place without meeting Swamiji who did not mind their parting. Bapuji was after Brahmanand. "Those three have left our place. I think you are compelling us to abuse you and throw you out." This threat hurt him very much. He came to me and said, "Mayaji, Om, I am going."

I said humbly, "Swamiji, we are at your service. Please forget whatever has been said by our elders." But he packed up his tiny bedding and left.

Accidently when he stepped out, he was confronted with Swamiji and Khudadad. They saw him in desparation and disgust. Swamiji enquired, "What is the matter?" The sanyasi replied, "I am going". Swamiji did not say anything else and allowed him to go.

On that day a Judge of Allahabad High Court, Mahabir Parsad, editor *Sarswati* and some other lawyers had come to stay with us.

Those guests had gone out for a walk. Standing in the court-yard Swamiji asked Khudadad, "You go to the residence of Ram Parsad engineer and request him to make arrangements for dinner. I am not prepared to take my meals at a place where a *sanyasi* is scolded and dishonoured." Khudadad replied, "I am going to ask him for arranging the dinner, but please don't get annoyed with your family members." After saying this, he accompanied Swamiji and stepped into our house.

Hardly had he reached the verandah, he picked up the lamp and threw it out. Khudadad asked him, "What are you doing?"

He slapped him and shouted, "Why aren't you leaving to make the dinner arrangements? It is not a home now but the abode of ghosts." Terrified Khudadad disappeared. Swamiji first broke the lamp, then picked up chairs and smashed them against the wall, reducing them into pieces. I was remembering the name of God and accompanying him fearing that he might smash his head against the wall. Then it was the turn of the clothes. He heaped them together, threw the beddings on it including his coat, sprinkled kerosene oil and set fire to them. The splendour on his face and the speed of his movements was indescribable. Then he turned toward the kitchen. He threw away the red-hot kettles with his hands, destroyed flour, pulses and all other eatables, kicked away the hearth and broke it. Terrified and helpless, his mother looked on silently.

At that moment the guests had returned from their walk. They were wonder-struck to see everything smashed and broken as though an earthquake had occurred. Smoke was coming out of the burnt clothes, broken chair pieces were scattered and the lamp with broken glass was lying on the ground.

Swamiji spoke in anguish and anger, "A *sanyasi* has been scolded, rebuked and dishonoured in this house. It is no longer a home, but a ghost's - abode where everything has become defiled."

All the guests fell on his feet and said, "Really you are a very great person. We could never imagine the amount of respect you hold for a *sanyasi.*"

My father-in-law ran in search of the sanyasi and was successful in tracing and bringing him back with humble request and with great difficulty. But Swamiji kept mum and did not talk to him. He left our place.

After doing all this, Swamiji became normal and undisturbed. A completely absorbed person considered his absorbability a real act of renunciation. The clouds in the rainy season always dominated his thinking process. Fully absorbed in that pensive mood he used to weep and sing:

I am itching for anything. Make me merry as much as you can.

Immediately he started reading out his essays to us. Dinner was provided to us by Ram Parshad engineer. We soon got engrossed in eating, laughing and singing for hours together. He sang:

At one time I was aware of the separation from my
  beloved,
But now there is neither the fairy nor my maina,
Thou art not thou, I am not I
.Only the bliss of ignorance is prevalent.

At that tlime my mother-in-law entered. She was feeling over-burdened and over-anguished for what had happened. "It is better you leave everybody and become a *sanyasi*". I felt intensely pained when I fully realized her mental torture as manifested by her saddened face. But whatever Swamiji did or wrote it was always under the spell of absorbability. It was impossible to describe his state of mind.

One evening we all were sitting. I was playing at the harmonium and singing. My voice perhaps appealed to one passer-by. He requested me to hand him over the harmonium. He played at the harmonium and sang:

> Don't distinguish between Ram and Allah
> Allow the True Almighty to rule your heart
> Always respond affirmatively to all
> This is the real secret of success in worldliness.

He sang this and disappeared. Neither we asked him his identity nor he cared to know anything about us. After that incident he never visited our house.

One day we all were sitting in our courtyard. One meek old lady with deep wrinkles on her wornout face, her stick trembling in her hand and having matted hair came and stood before Swamiji. After looking at the face of Swamiji, her eyes started sparkling and her face became subdued with smiles. She felt overrejoiced like a spiritual seeker who had been successful in having a glimpse of her master. Swamiji invited everybody present there to see that strange sparkle in her eyes. "The minds of all of you are only absorbed with her filthy stinking clothes, but at this moment the bliss of God Almighty is occupying her heart." He asked me, "Maya take her in, give her a bath, present her some neat pressed clothes and comb her hair tenderly." I immediately took her into the bathroom, washed her hair, gave her a thorough bath, applied oil on her hair, combed them properly and gave her a neat pressed suit to put on. After sometime I brought her out. Swamiji got her seated beside him, offered her tea to drink, blessed and embraced her. He repeated this sentence many a time, "At this moment the state of her blissful mind is that of a *yogi* (ascetic)." She left our house loaded with joy and pleasure.

That old lady came to our house once again when we all were sitting in a room. The peon informed Swamiji about her visit. "Turn her out and don't allow her to enter our house again," promptly came his answer.

"How is it that on that day you gave her all the honour and today so much disgrace to her?"

"You tell her that as people could not see the sparkle in her eyes on that day, today they cannot see the flaw in her heart."

Swamiji's heart and eyes worked like a weighing scale. His ears could discover the reality of one's voice. If anybody responded to his talk in an absent-minded way, he would become incensed and say, "Speak in your metallic voice which should sound ringing in the ears."

Master Amir Chand, Mian Khudadad, Hardial M.A. and Mr. Chatterji had identical viewpoints. They visited our place off and on. If any member of the party needed anything or money, he would ask Swamiji for that. They had instructed each other to get from Puran at Dehradun anything they needed. In this way, our house generally remained crowded. Kulkarni, a Maharashtrian and at one time a classfellow of Puran in Japan, was an anarchist. He lived in the Teehri state in disguise and was the leader of the revolutionary party. Whenever he was in need of money, he would come to our house at Dehradun. He had grown his beard and moustaches wildly. The governmental authorities were convinced that Puran was not a dangerous person.

One day we noticed somebody in our courtyard spying on us. Swamiji had a cane in his hand which he used freely on him making him unconscious. He came in and abused loudly the Britishers to his fill. Khudadad, who was sitting in his room, rushed to him. Swamiji narrated the whole episode of the spying person.

He thought that he would feel more agitated and enraged. He might even abuse the Britishers openly. He immediately went to the residence of Superintendent of Police and complained, "Why do you send your men at our residence for spying purposes?" He replied "It is done just for the protection of our Viceroy".

"Will it not be worse if every Indian starts despising every Britisher, than the killing of Viceroys one after the other?" spoke Khudadad in anguish and anger.

One day we all were sitting in the verandah. A hunter, with a big cage, full of red sparrows, came to our house. The helpless caged birds, in an effort to get free fluttered and dashed against the wall of the cage. Swamiji enquired of the hunter for the total amount he would like to charge for the whole lot. "Rupees thirty". He said. Swamiji asked me to bring thirty rupees. Swamiji offered the entire money to the hunter, but he was reluctant to accept it.

"I didn't mean this", the hunter said. Swamiji got agitated and shouted at him, "Open the cage". The hunter was so much terrified that he immediately opened the door of the cage. The caged birds, availing of the golden opportunity fluttered together to the door and briskly flying towards the sky disappeared in a second. This sudden flying of so many birds in a group gladdened Swamiji very much. A so called wise man was also sitting with us. He spoiled our whole pleasure. He said, "It was sheer wastage of money. The hunter will capture them again."

Swamiji shouted at him, "Get going, you don't deserve to be in our company."

The hunter went on grumbling for having accepted a short amount and the purely materialistic man went away with the grouse that Swamiji had wasted that money. But those who sincerely loved freedom were filled with the pleasure of enjoying the freeing of birds together. Even now that pleasant moment often haunts our minds.

Swamiji said, "Look Maya, the earth, water, and the manure are the same for all plants; but every seed extracts the food he needs for his nourishment. The mango extracts sweetness while the citrus fruits extract sourness. An expert gardener can get different fruits by properly grafting them. Similarly in this body-earth, there is a seed of unity which is formless. The colourless and formless spring of love is anxious to gush out but we have placed obstruction in its way in the form of our desires. The moment you remove the obstruction of your desires, the spring of love and unity will gush out. People coming into contact with you will completely quench their thirst and will rise to the heights of their meditation.

You can have His glimpse just by intuning your heart with Him

No travel is needed in this process.

At the time of giving such discourses, if any one moved his body or looked at someone else, Swamiji's concentration immediately got dissipated. He used to say, "You'd better go away, as you are not in a concentrative mood." He could forget himself and had the power to inspire others for completely forgetting themselves.

At Dehradun a boy by the name of Hari B.A. came to meet Swamiji. He said, "I belong to Kanpur and I am completely fed up with the atrocities committed on us by these Britishers."

He stayed with us for about six months and he explained to me one chapter titled *Khiskinda* of Tulsi Ramayana.

One day Hari narrated his whole story to Swamiji. "Somebody had sent me to you, as you were always helpful to needy persons like me. The police are after me but at present they are unaware of the fact that I am putting up with you. In fact I craved for going to Japan. Kindly help me by providing me fare to Japan and a letter of intoduction to someone known to you in that country". Swamiji agreed to help him.

But his photographs had been despatched to all the countries. He was able to contact the family for which Swamiji had given him the letter of introduction. Hari narrated his whole story to them. It was a law in Japan that if any immigrant got married to the daughter of some permanent resident, he automatically would become it's national. Hari was immediately married to their daughter. When the police came with orders of Hari's arrest issued by its Ambassador, they declared him their son-in-law. So the police became helpless and could not arrest him.

4. Dehradun

I was at Dehradun when Swamiji came back from Sardar Nagar. We had no prior information about his arrival. The moment he alighted from the tonga, he was terrifically enraged. I got depressed and none else dared ask him the reason for his anger. He started abusing without revealing the reasons for this provocation. When he calmed down he said, "Alas! I should not have gone to the sychophants of the Britishers." When I enquired of him about what the matter was, he replied in the same strain, "Now listen Maya, they have handed over those rooms where we had lived, to some English ladies whom they have employed to teach slavery to their children. They had broken our locks and had thrown away my books somewhere. They wanted to provide me a room under the stairs. If the servants go up, I had to bear the noise of their footsteps. When the landlords ascended the stairs, they created such a nasty noise as though horses were running. The children also created a lot of disturbance. The servants passed by my side belching loudly. I could neither read nor concentrate or write anything. I felt as if I was being hit on my head with shoes." After some days' rest he calmed down but still did not forget to abuse them. It seemed that he had been terrifically disturbed. Hardly had he recovered fully from that mental shock when he received letters from someone who had offered for rapprochment provided he was prepared to return to Suraya. This enraged him more. In reply to these letters he wrote back lengthy replies of fifty or sixty pages. I did not know what he wrote to him, but from his mood it was evident that he had taken a very hard and hostile stand.

Someone taunted him, "You took all the pains to grow the Rosha grass at Suraya, but they have ploughed all those fields for some other crops." He smiled and replied, "The sun showers light in abundance without caring whether the worldly people are utilizing it properly or not." He stayed at Dehradun and did not go.

In 1909, a large meeting was convened in the United Kingdom against Indians. Madan Lal Dhingra had shot dead an

Englishman by the name of Curzon. Dhingra belonged to their group. He was arrested. The moment his father came to know of his killing, he disinherited him from his property. The entire revolutionary party opposed and criticised him. They felt that this yoke of slavery hanging around the necks of Indians should be removed as early as possible. The Englishmen had been clever enough to influence and dominate our sentiments and emotions. No one in the world would ever remember India as a country. If these brave Indian militants were allowed to be executed, then there would be no hope for India's freedom. So all the revolutionaries became alert and active to compel the Britishers to quit India before they were able to crush our self-respect and integrity.

Hardial wrote to me, "Sister, time had come when the countrymen were to be awakened from their slumber and were inspired for making sacrifices." He reached Dehradun soon and informed us that all of them were going to disguise themselves in the garb of *sanyasis* (ascetics) and he would hang a bell around him so that people might call him the ascetic with a bell.

At Delhi they held secret meetings to plan the killings of Britishers. They prepared so many papers for despatch to other places. But those papers were recovered and confisticated. Most of those papers were written in Hardial's handwriting and so he was declared a rebel. When he came to know of this fact, he visited our place at Dehradun. I served him with water and some eatables but he refused to take anything saying, "I will accept nothing from your home, because Puran is in the service of the British Government." I replied, "But had he not been in service here, how could we provide you with this protection? Moreover, I am not a government servant but only in a household job. So I must get some pay for this service. I am offering you these eatables out of that income. Kindly accept them."

He said, "By killing that bastard Englishman, Madan Lal Dhingra has saved India's honour." To this I said, "We also belong to that category."

During that interval our son came to that room. He took him into his arms and said, "We will appoint him the Viceroy of India."

On that very day Hardial left our place without disclosing his destination. But within a few days he was arrested at Delhi and exiled to the United Kingdom.

Hardial had been visiting us for a long time. He stood first in the M.A. examination of the University and got a scholarship for going abroad. One day he asked me, "To which European country should I go?" I advised him to go to United Kingdom. He replied, "But mangoes are not available there." "Then you better go to America." I said, "But *ganderris* (small cuttings of the sugarcane) are not available there." (But poor fellow got the punishment of exilement).

Hardial had sent a message to Khudadad through somebody to make arrangements for sending his wife abroad.

But Hardial's in-laws never allowed him to enter their premises. The husband and wife used to meet each other at some secret place and Hardial had introduced Khudadad to her and they had met each other several times. At the time of his exilement, he had sent a message to her that Khudadad would take her to him. She belonged to a kayasth family and had never gone alone to any place. But for the sake of her husband she took all her ornaments and cash and met Khudadad at a pre-decided place. Khudadad, posing himself as a Muslim provided her with a *burqa* (mantle) for disguising herself. But her mother got the scent of her daughter's elopement.

The mother entreated to her sons, "Your sister has left our house for meeting Hardial. After his exilement, she used to weep bitterly for her husband."

Her brothers reported the matter to the Superintendent of Police who wired to all railway authorities to make special efforts for her arrest. Her brothers searched all trains but she narrowly escaped from their search. After sending her abroad, Khudadad came back to Dehradun and clasped Swami Puran so tightly and closely as if they were two bodies with one spirit in them.

It was an October night, when myself, Swamiji and Khudadad were sitting under the canopy of a starry sky and were under the spell of our concentrations. Tears of love and affection were coming out of Swamiji's eyes. He said, "You have fully lived to the expectations of Hardial. Please narrate the incidents of your secret journey in detail." He narrated to us the whole awful situations of their journey packed with suspense and fear. Immensely pleased with his achievement, Swamiji said, "Maya, in the presence of this enchanting nature, I entrust this saintly son to you". Placing his head in my motherly lap, he said, "Please bestow him with an affectionate kiss."

Intoxicated with this new relationship, we sat there for hours together in that ecstasy. This relationship developed into a permanent feature and remained so for fifty three years when we lived together under the same roof.

In 1910 Khudadad went to Germany for his higher studies in Chemistry. But the other revolutionaries kept on visiting us. Many people used to come to us, most of them having no means of livelihood. Glandened with the zeal of unity from Swamiji and a spirit of service on my part, they returned to their assigned duties with full satisfaction. All the revolutionaries used to talk in my presence without any reservation.

Once a Japanese came for espionage and to collect secrets of the Britishers. He stayed with us for a full one year.

All Swamiji's relatives had great affection for him. His elder sister Lajan was married to Teja Singh who was a post master and a staunch Sikh. Since Puran Swami did not don long hair, neither did Teja Singh visit his in-laws, nor did he allow his wife to go to her parents. But Lajan often compelled him to allow her to meet her parents. Sometimes she stayed with us for full two years along with her children and did not go back to him unless called by him.

In 1910 her son contacted typhoid while she was with us. The doctors attending on him lost all hopes for his recovery and Teja Singh was telegraphically informed accordingly with the request to come. But he did not visit our place and instead wrote a letter that he would not come to that house, where a fallen Sikh was residing. If the boy dies, burn him there. But somehow the doctors could save the boy. Sister Lajan felt very much dejected. She entreated to her mother, "If my brother agrees to wear long hair, I will be saved from all this harassment and frustration". Her mother replied with the same determination, "I care too hoots for the Sikhs and your husband. My son is a much better Sikh than those people."

Lajan received many letters from her husband entreating her to return and she went back to Sialkot.

But in April 1912, when Swamiji met Bhai Vir Singh at the Sialkot session of the Sikh Conference, he felt a miraculous impact of his magnetic personality. Sir Joginder Singh, who was the President of the Sikh Conference at Sialkot had great affection for Swamiji. He wrote to Swamiji, "Please do attend the Sikh Conference at Sialkot." Swamiji agreed to attend the session. It was a very big Sikh gathering. Sir Joginder Singh requested Swamiji to give a discourse. Inspired by the presence of thousands of Sikhs in their traditional attire, Swamiji spoke with zest and vigour and the audience listened to him with rapt attention. After finishing with his lecture, when he came back to take his seat on the dias, Bhai Vir Singh asked him to sit beside him. Enamoured of his speech, he patted him with pleasure and for blessing him, he moved his hand on his head. "Your hair are very soft and silky, quite contrary to those having hard and stiff shorn hair." He then took Swamiji along with him to his place of stay and they took their meals together. They kept on talking for hours together and did not care to have some rest. For the whole evening they remained in each other's company and at night dined together. They remained busy in exchanging notes till late at night. Next night Swamiji boarded a train for Dehradun. Now he was a completely changed and transformed man. He was in a deep pensive mood. Ultimately he told me, "I have decided to wear long hair. I will not allow anybody to cut my hair which have been touched and blessed by Bhai Vir Singh."

I was engrossed with many misgivings. At present only Teja Singh was objecting to his shorn hair, but if he desecrated his long hair again, there would be a huge hue and cry in the society. I did not utter a single word in this connection. Bhai Sahib wrote him lengthy letters and he in reply was doing the same. There was a miraculous change in his temperament.

The government had a leprosy centre at Dehradun. Off and on he took me to that place, loaded with sweets and fruits. He helped patients in taking those eatables. We used to feel overjoyed when we noticed blossoming smiles of satisfaction and pleasure on their faces. He would help someone to eat a bannana and sweets to those whose hands could not move. I also felt inspired in doing this kind of service to them and the impulse of untouchability never came into my way.

I had all along been appreciating his gesture of embracing patients suffering from tuberculosis. None else seemed to have enjoyed the pleasure out of his such strange gesture as I did because he had been inspiring me to live above the petty feelings of contempt and hatred.

Once an acquaintance of ours, very beautiful indeed, was suffering from tuberculosis. We were at Dehradun and she had no real and personal sympathiser to look after her. Her backbone got affected. She sent me a message, with an urgent appeal to see her before her death as her days were numbered. I went to my parents at Ralwalpindi and immediately proceeded to her house. I straight went to her room and embraced her. Tuberculosis had completely shattered her health, eclipsing her moon-like beauty. She responded to my affectionate embrace with her trembling arms and spoke in a very feeble voice, "My dear sister, a strange stench is coming out of my body and everybody shudders on entering my room. You may also kindly go out of my room." Consoling her I said, "Sita, love-embrace always gives out a pleasing fragrance, while only lustful-embrace emits odour. You may kindly forget all these considerations and only love me."

I arranged a maid-servant for her and got sprayed many scents in her room. A daily visit to her was a must for me. In this way a few days passed peacefully. Her sparkling eyes always attracted me. I was beside her till her death. At that time these couplets flashed upon my inward eye.

> This cage gets rust and rotten,
> But not the soul-bird.
> This cage gets shattered
> But the bird's beauty remains untarnished.
> Don't mistake the body for the soul,
> Such body never blossoms with youth
> Birds, flying to farthest heights,
> Are not tempted by earthly attractions.

I got this feeling of true and spiritual love only through Swamiji's blessings. He used to say, "Maya, this wide-world is limitless. We need not be conscious of our limitations". He once sang,

> All barriers of duties, needs and diseases
> Are shattered with one stroke of Death,
> As all excesses and cruelties are,
> Levelled with a drawing plank.

He had no worry for the future. Regarding the amassing of wealth, he thought it to be just collecting of filth. Learn lessons from the liberality of Nature which freely distributes its wealth with both hands. The rivers are flowing swiftly, full of water for free distribution to all. Darkness, mute darkness at night is all over for all. The trees germinate millions of seeds free for all: no doubt all seeds do not turn into plants, but their distribution is totally free. The fast flowing rivers quench the thirst of their fellow trees, fields and other living human beings without any reservation or discrimination. We see water, water everywhere on this earth. In comparison to this just see this small pond keeping all its water to itself. After sometime this very fresh water will stagnate into stench that nobody would like to come near it or drink a drop of its water. Will anybody like to have a bath in this water full of foul smell? Rather this very idea looks ridiculous. Similarly you cannot tolerate the company of a greedy person who had amassed wealth because you know that he could not be of any help to you. A slave of money counting - course dare not donate anything to anyone. A man gets ennobled and fresh by coming into contact with liberal and generous people. He always recited this couplet:

> I am sprinkling colours in abundance,
> On the variegated people of this world
> The game of colours is in full swing
> And I have drenched them through and through.

Pointing towards the sun, he used to say, "Look Maya, just see the liberal and free distribution of the sun, which goes even to caves, so that those are not deprived of this free bliss. Distribute freely and liberally whatever you have with you."

> If your love for Him is pure and true
> Need not save a penny for your coffin.

Whosoever was at that time in his company, he would enrich him with his valuable views.

Gargi was an infant child in those days. She used to often wonder about his remarks, "Distribute your wealth liberally." Poor girl did not have enough dolls to play with even. One day she asked her father, "Dad, when shall we have plenty of money? You liberally distribute all that you have."

He replied, "My dear daughter, one day there will be a rain of rupees all over and all roads and courtyard will be filled with rupees. These rupees are dirty, which we don't want to save for you."

Gargi said, "At the time of rain of rupees if I pick them up you will say my daughter is collecting scattered and uncared material from the streets." Listening to her interesting talks he laughed and said, "You are perfectly right my darling."

Once my two nieces came to us at Dehradun. Shakuntala was studying in a convent school but poor Hariyan (Harbans) was totally uneducated. Both were unmarried. Coming back from his Forest College, he used to sit with them over a cup of tea and enjoy their entertaining talks. When they found some difference in their amounts of money, they used to quarrel with each other. Swamiji fully enjoyed their quarrels.

After reaching home, he used to provoke them for a quarrel. I also used to laugh with them, but could not leak out to them his views about money. One day he was explaining to some one, "All this wealth, ornaments and rupees are filth. With their possession, one loses one's balance of mind." A girl was listening to his discourse. She suggested to him, "You better throw this filth in our house." He retorted, "Why should we do that? We will rather sweep out your filth also and throw it out." Someone sitting with him had a heartiest laugh over this interesting situation and remarked, "You wanted to have his share but he, instead of giving you his share, will rather deprive you of your own."

The factory at Dohiwala, where we are putting up these days was under construction. People living there, told me that Swamiji used to visit the construction site off and on. The chimney of the factory is eighty four feet high. When the masons and the labourers were constructing it, he would look at them working at such a huge height by bending his head backwards. He used to bring for them bags full of walnuts and distribute them liberally among them. If he felt any irritation in his ear, he would take out a note, may be of any denomination, roll it for use in the ear and throw the same on the ground. The labourers nearby used to run to pick up the same and sometimes started quarrelling amongst themselves. Labourers working at the top of the chimney looked helplessly but he used to compensate them by giving them a rupee each.

Swamiji had reserved some first floor rooms for the purpose of his writing — some to elevate him to the realms of love and others to take him to the farthest heights of poetry. With the abundance of emotions in him, he could easily touch those high limits. He felt terribly disturbed when he heard someone's harsh and greedy voice. He had to come down completely shaken and shattered. He felt so much enraged that he would break into pieces anything lying beside him — may be a dinner set or tea set. Nobody could understand the reason for his doing this sudden act, but I could fully realize how perturbed he must be feeling for his mental disturbance and disturbed concentration.

When he was able to reach the farthest heights of the realms of poetry, he used to compose his poems and recite them. Tears started dripping out of his eyes. Anybody sitting beside him could also enjoy that feeling of ecstasy at that moment. This state of mind was not conditioned to any particular place or situation. But if anyone disturbed his concentration by complaining about less use of salt in some dish, he would feel terribly angered and dash all the utensils around him.

Swamiji had no faith in ill-omens. Rather he was an optimistic person always radiating the rays of hopes and transforming others under that spell.

Swamiji took strong objections to enchanters and those who claimed the power to exercise or believe in mortification. He used to say, "What mortification had Gaja (a mythological elephant) undertaken?"

Neither virtue nor any education,
Gaj could perform the religious deeds.

An enchanter could impress him only for a few days. Discovering his other mean and dirty habits worst than that of an ordinary man, he would discard him for ever.

In December 1917 a Bengali woman Sarla Devi, wife of Barrister Rambhaj Dutt, came to see him at night. Her dazzling beauty was inspiring and faultless as if specially carved by a sculpture out of a stone. Her costly sari with her shining ornaments bedecked with pearls and jewels added to her beauty. At that time we were taking our dinner. The moment she entered our room, she fell on Swamiji's feet and started weeping bitterly. Swamiji got up and helped her to stand on her feet. She embraced Swamiji while weeping and said, "My heart is burning. Please bestow upon me some peace of mind." He blessed her and said, "Your misery is because of the duality in you. The root cause of your heart - burning is your temperament surrounded by desires and temptations." He explained to her how we can purify our mind with the feelings of unity, love and sacrifice. His discourse had a miraculous effect on her and she closed her eyes. It seemed as if Sarla Devi's body had become lifeless and motionless. After sometime she stood on her feet, fully relaxed and over-intoxicated with peace and joy. She thanked Swamiji and left our place. When she had gone, Swamiji said, "I have become void. I have donated all my pleasures and joys to her. Bitten by duality and surrounded by her desires, she has looted all my valuables. Then he started singing and went on doing so far sometime.

Beware my friend, it is a swindler's world,
Your slight carelessness may cost you the
whole of your merchandise.

Swamiji's mother belonged to a Malik family. Pleased with their useful and sincere services to the government, the authorities gifted them a big village which was christened as Dera Khalsa. It was a romantic village. A very deep rivulet flowed between the two hills of Kumbhi and Kumiali. It's whole area was mountainous, full of greenery on all sides and some ravines flowing with water.

Other than Maliks, some people in the village worked as their land-tenants. So most of the daughters of the Malik families were generally married to the sons of these land-tenants. These ladies had an upper hand in the homes of their in-laws. They used to stay with their parents as much time as they wished to. They were proud of the fact that they belonged to the families of the landlords. Swamiji's mother, belonging to the Malik family lived most of her life with her parents. His mother, leaving her son Puran in the custody of her mother, used to spend her whole day in singing and dancing with her friends. So Swamiji was brought up with great fondling and was lucky enough to enjoy the natural beauty of that area. For most part of his childhood he lived at his maternal grandfather's house. His maternal uncle had great love for him and kept him in his company most of the time. His maternal uncle was very fond of meeting and talking to saintly persons.

Swamiji enjoyed the company of saints, played with them, listened to their discourses and sometimes even passed certain sarcastic remarks about them. They enjoyed and laughed at his innocent but intelligent remarks and used to say, "One day he will reveal his queerness to the world." Interestingly amongst those saints there was one ascetic who was known by the name of 'tappi'. He used to take Swamiji in his lap and intoxicated with the warmth of his love, he would look at his sparkling eyes for hours together. He generally remarked, "He is a marvellous man and I will witness his queerness with my own eyes." This ascetic was so strong that he used to stand amidst the fast flowing water of the Attak river in the morning for hours together till the sun rose. He would look at the sun for sometime and dip himself into its turbulent water and swim across the river.

He used to practise many more mortifications. When he came to know that Puran had become a *sanyasi* (ascetic) while living with his family, he was immensely pleased. He had an urgent desire of meeting Puran. Asking many people of his whereabouts, one day he reached Dehradun. Though he had grown very old, yet he had a strong and a ringing voice. Both of them immediately recognised each other. Gladdened with the sight, he clasped Puran Swami tightly. He felt intoxicated when he looked at Swamiji's sharp sparkling eyes continuously for sometime without batting his eyelid.

This ascetic had become an accomplished saint and a divine personage. He had the supernatural power of going anywhere or seeing anything. People followed him wherever he went. Immediately after arriving at our place, he informed us about his diet and sleep. "I need one room to myself. For my bath arrange one maund of ice for cooling the water, cook four *saer* (nearly four kilo) of meat with one *saer* of ghee (vegetable oil), bring one bottle of superior whisky. I will go to sleep at ten at night and will open my door next day at four in the evening."

We continued overhearing for the whole night different voices from his room. Sometimes it was a commanding voice, at times as if some were listening to the voice of a mendicant. At other moments the fluttering-sound of birds was heard from the room. Many of his followers, when they came to know of his whereabouts, flocked to Dehradun and helped him in a thorough bath in the evening. After his bath with the cold water he used to sit in his room surrounded by his followers and would listen to their requests, promising to help them to their satisfaction. He used to take his complete diet of meat and whisky to his heart's content after his bath. Some followers complained of having lost their sons, elopement of their wives with their paramours or having lost their precious belongings in thefts. This ascetic, after achieving his concentration for some moments, used to tell his believers where their lost sons were roaming or where their wives were. Sometimes he used to call back their lost sons to their houses. But his miraculous feats did not impress us. Swamiji did not cherish these supernatural feats to be performed in his house, but he, being his well-wisher and blesser since his childhood, kept mum. Swamiji did not talk to him on any issue. He left our place after staying with us for a month.

By temperament Swamiji was very impatient. He wanted that every work of his should be completed immediately and in no time. Bibi Harnam Kaur from Nabha came to us with her manuscript *Arshi Kaliyan* and requested Swamiji for writing an introduction for the same. She had expressed her desire to Swamiji late at night at the dining table. We went on talking to her till eleven at night and then everybody left for bed.

Swamiji immediately started penning down the introduction for her book *Arshi Kaliyan* and completed it by twelve o'Clock that night. Inspired by its completion, he came with the introduction and called aloud, "Oh Biria, oh Biria, come on and listen to the introduction I have just now completed." Dr. Balbir Singh replied, "May I praise the merits of your introduction after listening to it or even without listening?" Swamiji realised that Dr. Balbir Singh was not in a mood to listen to his introduction with his sleepy mind. "Alright admire it now and listen to it in the morning."

At Dehradun one evening Sardarni Sant Kaur Oberoi came to us and said to Swamiji, "Since Lala Urgra Sen is known to you, kindly get the building plan of our bungalow approved. Swamiji agreed to it and she handed over the building plan to him.

It was summer. Next day at about five in the morning she sent her servant to enquire whether their building plan had been approved. He did not say anything to the servant but went in and brought her building plan. Addressing Dr. Balbir Singh he said, "Oh Biria, Oh Biria, I accept my defeat. There are people in this world who are much more impatient than me."

Swamiji was very fond of cleanliness. We had a small servant boy whose primary duty was to kill flies. In one hand he kept the fly-swat and in the other a small box in which he threw the flies after killing them. Not to say of rooms, we could not find a single fly in the courtyard. One day I was sitting in the compound. Suddenly Swamiji called me aloud, "Maya, Come in, Maya, come in immediately." Bewildered, I ran to his room where he was writing something. I asked, "What is the matter?" He said, "She has entered my room." "Who?" I asked in the same sense of bewilderment.

"A fly has after all entered in the room."
"But she is not a lioness that you cried so aloud?"

Smilingly he said, "it was just a pretext to call you in." Now when I narrate this interesting incident to our grandchildren they enjoy it very much and very often request me again and again to regale them with the repetition of this narration.

We never discussed household problems with each other. If any interesting incident which had happened at Rawalpindi flashed upon my mind and haunted me for narration to him, he used to get enraged and often say, "Your soul is still at Rawalpindi. What is the fun of keeping your body here at Dehradun?" In this way he helped me in avoiding all de-concentrating ideas in my mind; rather he suggested to me the methods for achieving complete concentration of mind and not allowing the mind to go astray. I always valued his suggestions and enjoyed in practising them. In this way my mind felt easy, clear and concentrated.

Days passed on in achieving concentration, unity and oneness through service. Swamiji always helped and inspired me in elevating myself in self-realization. He guided me in avoiding duality, hatred and grumbling in life.

I was always at his service. I kept myself busy in getting flour grinded and cooking meals for him. Nothing else could disturb me in any way.

5. Patiala

In 1918 Swami Puran Singh, having developed some grouse with the government, resigned his post from the Forest Research Institute, Dehradun. But the conservator of the forest felt that an exceptionally intelligent person like Puran Singh was being ill-treated. He advised Swami Puran Singh to take back his resignation and if he did not want to continue with the job, to appear before a Medical Board for a medical examination. "Since you are not keeping good health, you can easily have the benefit of your pension," he said. In those days Swamiji was suffering from albumen and gout. The Medical Board recommended his case and a pension was sanctioned in his favour.

After that Swamiji agreed to seek service with the Maharaja of Patiala. I had a disliking for these states. I frankly told him, "Neither I will go to this State nor will I accept any amount from your State - earning." But he had his own whims. So he joined his service at Patiala. After two months he posted me an insured letter for Rupees three thousand, which I refused to accept. I also wrote to him that I was not prepared to accept anything from this earning.

Swamiji had started working at his office at Patiala and had recruited his staff also. After five months he left everything at Patiala and one day returned to Dehradun without meeting the Maharaja of Patiala. He said, "Maya, your prediction was correct. I felt suffocated at Patiala."

One day he received a letter from a clerk of his office. "We had heard that jackals enjoy the lion's prey to their heart's content. You had provided us with your prey and for the last nine months we were doing nothing but getting our salaries regularly."

After returning from Patiala, he went to Bombay. At Bombay he signed an agreement with a richman and brought those papers to Dehradun. It was winter and we were sitting near a burning furnace. He read out to me the contents of the agreement. I knew pretty well that he could not work with any body. I took those papers from him and threw them into the fire. It was about seven in the evening. He was very much enraged. He ordered me to get out of his house.

I retorted, "It is my house and I will not go out of it." He spoke in the same mood, "Alright, I will quit it. I kept mum because I knew that if I said anything to him, he would be furious and might go out of his limits with anger. He ordered the servant to go and fetch one carriage from Adams, who used to give his carriages on hire. When the carriage arrived, he kept his books in a box and left the place.

In those days an engineer by the name of Abbasi was staying with us. When he came back he enquired of Swamiji. I narrated the whole incident to him. He hired the very same carriage in which Swamiji had left and asked the driver to take him to the place where he had dropped Swamiji. He took him to the house of Lala Ugra Sen. Abbasi said to Lala Ugra Sen, "Our thief has come to your place and why have you hidden him?"

He replied, "My dear, he is elder to me and I have no choice but to obey him." All of them laughed to their heart's content and Swamiji returned home in that very carriage with Abbasi. After reaching home, he said, "I was expecting that Maya would dissuade me from leaving the house, but she did not ask me even once."

He never commanded me; rather he expected service from me for the love I had for him. He considered my service invaluable. He even did not cherish to hear from me "I will do what you desire me to do". If at certain moments I uttered these words unconsciously, he would retort immediately, "You are still an unbaked pot and consider me a master of my slaves." He wanted me to develop my indepedent individuality. He used to say, "One should always feel fully independent" He would not allow even complete independence to be a sort of bondage for anyone. His heart was like a balancing-scale which could not bear the slightest weight of a hair. Through his varied and rich experience, he had developed his capability of judging people properly and judiciously. He did not have the slightest faith in ill-omens and had trained me accordingly. He treated me as his sincere life-companion. He always tried to develop in me a feeling of oneness and tested me several times for the same.

One English lady, who was acquainted to us was putting up in our house. She had a pregnant pet-bitch with her. At dead of night, the bitch gave birth to her cubs. The English lady ran to me and said, "Mrs Puran Singh, kindly provide me with a box where I may keep her cubs safely." I thought for a moment because all the boxes were in the storeroom, which was outside and near the kitchen. Immediately I recollected that one box was lying over the almirah in the bathroom. When I picked up that box, a chandan wood, five feet long and quite heavy lying in the box, fell upon my foot and crushed my toe miserably. Blood gushed out of it, but in spite of my bleeding toe, I handed over the box to her. I also provided her with bread and milk for the bitch. Blood from my thumb kept on dripping on the carpets. I sat on my cot and extending my foot away from the bed, I pressed my toe. I made no noise lest Swamiji should feel perturbed. But he woke up and enquired, "What's the matter?" I replied, "I have got an injury on my foot."

He advised me to apply tincture, which I did immediately. But blood kept oozing. "Why are you sitting?" he asked me and switched on the light. He noticed a small pool of blood near the cot and angrily asked, "Why didn't you cry?"

Unconsciously I replied, "The Sikh spirit does not allow us to cry in pain." He got furious and condemned the Sikh spirit in unspeakable terms. "What is this sikh-spirit which prompts its adherants to sacrifice principles of life? Had you cried, I would have myself applied tincture to your toe and would have served you with milk or water. See the quantity of blood that has dripped out. Your Sikh-spirit which prevents another man from service to his companion is absolutely wrong. You have been cruel to me by not informing me in time." He did not talk to me for the whole week.

6. Gwalior

Swamiji accidently met the Raja of Gwalior at Delhi in a meeting. Impressed by the views and personality of Swamiji, he requested Swamiji to come to Gwalior and start work there. Swamiji told him frankly, "If you are prepared to advance Rupees Twenty five thousand for the education of my children and deposit Rupees two lakhs in my name, only then I will work in your state. You, rulers of states initially are keen to employ somebody but later on completely forget him."

Raja Scindia agreed to all his conditions and as desired by Swamiji he sent him Rupees twenty five thousand and deposited Rupees two lakhs in his name. At Gwalior he was provided with an official bungalow, a car and a chauffeur. A staff was recruited for the project. He was able to produce such things in the state, as could not be grown in that area. He planted Rosha grass and the saplings of eucalyptus. For the proper growth of those tender plants, arrrangements were made for protecting them with the sheets of *khas khas* (Cymbopogon arometicus). For watering those sheets, water carriers were recruited. He started the manufacturing of shellac wax, as its water was helpful in the growth of eucalyptus plants. So he was able to show miracles as if he had an Allaudin's lamp with him. Within a year the eucalyptus trees rose to the height of eight feet.

Whenever he went to his royal court, the Raja used to ask him to sit beside him and not amongst his courtiers. He used to ask him about his progress in Rosha grass. Swamiji told him that he had started their sale in the market. One hundred pounds of it had been despatched to Bombay. Even shellac wax was being sold in the market.

Rupees two lakhs, which he had deposited in the name of Swamiji, had exhausted and further budgetary provisions were to be made for this project. People had complained to the Raja that no doubt, Sardar Sahib was a very honest and sincere person, but his subordinates, taking undue advantage of his trust reposed in them, were misusing the money. When

Swamiji raised the question of his further granting the money, the Raja replied, "I fully trust you, but your subordinates are misusing the money."

The moment the Raja uttered these words, Swamiji got furious and shouted at him, forgetting the etiquettes of the royal court, "Look Scindia, you have only ears to listen. I was under the impression that you were like the old Rajas of the states, but you have proved yourself quite otherwise."

Raja replied, "Alright, do you think that I have only ears? Am I ruling my entire state with my ears?" Swamiji retorted, "I repeat my statement thousand times that you have no intellect but only ears." Raja Scindia got reddened with anger. But God knows why he, under the spell of Swamiji, did not say anything. He nodded for the closure of the royal court.

Observing all sorts of etiquettes, all courtiers left that royal court. Swamiji also sat in the car and returned to his residence. He ordered his servant to put all his manuscripts in a box and dashed towards the railway station in the car. He took the next available train and reached Dehradun. Everybody left rejoiced by his presence. Nobody asked him anything. He awakened Khudadad saying, "Oh Bhapa (brother), Oh Bhapa! just see the quality of work I had done there. Come on, I will narrate my whole story to all of you." Addressing me he said, "Maya darling, you were correct in your prediction. Gwalior is just like other states." He fully enjoyed the whole narration of his story and started singing.

> Enjoy your life and love your God.
> May you prosper and don silky garments.

He felt greatly relieved and happy after leaving the service of the Raja. There were great rejoicings in the whole family.

> Prosperity is everywhere, fortunate I am,
> My hunger and desire have been won over,
> I play with the stars in the sky,
> My kite is flying on the farthest heights,
> And that too without any thread.
> I am blessed with precious golden wristlets,
> The moments my glass-bangles got broken
>   (Swami Ram).

"Oh Maya, just imagine the stupendous task I have performed. Order for sweets. I have taught the Raja such a lesson as he would not have learnt before. I am dead sure he dare not misbehave with a saint in future."

The Raja of Gwalior wrote to him four letters entreating for a meeting but he did not go to meet him. The Raja remitted him a full year's salary at Dehradun.

At Gwalior he wrote a lot. Since he had been in correspondence with many European countries, he had purchased many books, which could hardly be stocked in four big almirahs. Except his books he did not touch anything of his house at the time of his departure from Gwalior. Many people suggested to him to arrange the despatch of the costly carpets which he had left behind at Gwalior But he always said,

> Their possession was taken to whom they belonged,
> Mahiwal fully feels relieved.

Similarly if he had lost his manuscripts he would not mind it much. On somebody's enquiry, he used to say, "Just look at a tree which has innumerable seeds, but all of them do not grow into plants. Rather some of them are scattered hither and thither. People do not like *calotropis gigantea,* but nature has provided its seeds the power to fly."

Raja had instructed his state-musicians and painters to obey Puran Singh's orders without getting prior permission from any one. Mr. Munshi was very good at music and used to come to Puran Singh everyday for an hour or so. Swamiji used to try to learn the songs sung by him with the help of a harmonium a thing which otherwise irritated him. He used to reject it by saying, "This damn instrument has multifarious tunes, which create so many different sounds." But he was a real lover of music. So he tried to transcribe the rhymes and rhythms of 'Lachhi' songs into poetry. This relates to December 1923, when these 'Lachhi' folk songs had recently become popular and people loved to sing them even while walking on the roads. One couplet had an immense appeal for Puran Singh and he very often sang it :

On one side Lachhi cherishes milk,
But on the other, shatters alien's glasses to pieces.

There were about fifteen people staying in our house in those days and we all sang this song collectively, echoing it into a full fledged chorus. Our singing-voice and smiling-noise, crossed the precincts of our house and could be heard even from the adjacent road.

He could not tolerate any cuttings in his writings. From Gwalior he wrote to me, "I have composed a song on Lachhi but I always have the apprehension that someone might make corrections in it or disfigure it by cutting its nose and ears."

Swamiji wrote to me the following letter concerning the poetry of Lacchi songs.

"Yes, I have written an introduction comprising twenty pages about Lachhi, in which I have discussed in details why I have selected the name of Lachhi. There are no special qualities in this folk song which has attracted the attention of so many people. But a buffalo - like bulky and black introduction that I have written is really very good.

"I hope to finish this book within ten days. Everyday I keep on writing whatever Munshi sings before me. I think it will run into approximately fifty pages."

He was very keen to have a feeling of love for others. He cared for the smallest wish of the person whom he loved. Swamiji could live only in the realm of love. He completed 'Lachhi' with an introduction of twenty pages and all its songs covered only forty pages. I just remember the following lines from his songs:

Citron has blossomed in Panjab
But away is my beloved,
Oh! Lachhiye, adorn a handful of citrons,
Your odour will have its desired effect on us.

Loaded with enthusiasm, he left for Amritsar with Lachhi and read it out to many people who appreciated it very much. But when he saw it in print and heard a slight hint of disappreciation, he went down, dismantled the whole frames of type and tore out all the printed papers. I was an eyewitness to all this. Then he came up and declared, "I have burnt it down". But I did not utter a single word.

After sometime he enquired, "What had happened Maya? Did I say anything?" I kept mum. Inwardly I heaved a sigh. "Alas! a wonderful piece of poetry has met its death." Then a few couplets which he used to sing flashed upon my inward eye and made me calm and quiet :

I have neither desire nor feeling of search,
Without worship, I have no ambition big or small,
When my inward-eye opened through liberation,
Oh beloved, I find you everywhere and in front
of me.

After destroying Lachhi which he had sung and written for months together, he left for Gwalior. He wrote to me a lengthy letter that he was always after his lost Lachhi. This happened in the summer of 1924.

Once in 1922 we were all having our morning tea at Gwalior.

Madanmohan Singh filled his cup to the brim. When somebody remarked about how selfish he was he said, "I have filled the cup for Gargi." I recollected an old incident which I narrated to all.

It relates to 1898 when *tongas* (coaches drawn by horses) were available for Koh Marri (Murri hills). Those *tongas* were owned by Panjhi Bhai and a pair of horses was changed after every ten miles. Even up to Kashmir these coaches were made available. One man drove through this coach after having his rest at a certain resting places. We all (myself, my brother Bhakat Sain Dass, his wife and mother) left for Kohmarri in a *tonga*. We reached Ghoragalli where there was a small shop at the road-side. Tea and meals were generally made available for the passengers. It was eleven in the morning. My brother went to place an order for the meals. There used to be a middle-aged man with his boy-servant. But he saw a young damsel roaming in the maize crop at the rear part of the house. He enquired of her, "Where is the shopkeeper? We want meals immediately as we are to proceed further."

The girl replied, "I have no time for cooking meals." But strangely enough she was making all arrangements for cooking a meal. When Bhakatji insisted, "Kindly provide us with meals, as we are very hungry," she admonished him saying, "Sit outside the shop why have you come in?" Bhakatji was of a very shy nature. The poet has described him in his poem *"Ik Jangli Phul'* as "a person with a vacant heart." Without uttering a single word, he came out of the shop and silently sat on the bench outside. We were sitting at a very vantage point from where we could easily watch the rear portion of the house. Bhakatji noticed that a young man visited her several times and then vanished in the maizecrop. Bhakatji felt very shy and turned his face on the other side as he had fully visualized the whole situation. By that time the shopkeeper, clad in dirty old clothes, entered the shop and admonishing her asked, "What are you doing? What's all this?" He had noticed that somebody had vanished in the maize-crop.

She said, "the brother sitting outside the shop has ordered for *parathas* stuffed with potatoes." Then she called him, "Come on brother and have your meal. We are already late in complying with your order."

The moment Swamiji heard this narration, the poet in him got very much inspired and his imaginative faculty reached the farthest heights. Saturated with his poetic-faculty, he immediately started writing his long-poem "Ik Jangli Phul' which later on was included in *Khule Maidan.*

The Engagement of our Daughter Gargi

Whenever there was a family gathering, the issue of Gargi's marriage used to crop up. One day we received a letter from Gwalior that Swamiji had come across an intelligent young man to whom he wanted to propose for Gargi. That young man was totally unknown to us. I wrote to him back not to proceed further in the matter as we would like to select a young man from our family. When he received my letter, he sent a telegram to his brother's wife Sant Kaur, asking her to send a word of congratulation to the parents of Malik Amar Singh. Nobody in the family was consulted and the boy and the girl had not seen each other even once. At that time the boy

GWALIOR

was studying for his M.Sc. We received a telegram from Rawalpindi that Gargi had been engaged to Malik Amar Singh and they were rejoicing the occasion.

This telegram from Gargi's uncle surprised us all. We also received a telegram from Gwalior that the engagement of Gargi had been finalized with Malik Amar Singh. "Please accept my congratulations." He also wrote a letter to Gargi, which was written in English and was a wonderful piece of poetry. It is given below:

My dear daughter,

I have decided to love you, serve you and dedicate my whole self to you. You have to be more active, more spiritual and more loving from today for developing your sense of service, sacrifice and love. Otherwise this whole exercise will go waste. Life is God and we have to realize that our spirit is God and an element of God. God has bestowed us days and nights just to recognize ourselves.

I hope you will excuse me for saying that this human body is the temple of God. To be careless about it is to defile it. I had no knowledge of it when I started my life-career, otherwise I would have preferred to serve this temple of God. Being my daughter you have exactly followed me and have been quite careless towards it. Our ancestors used to offer only that horse for sacrifice at the worship-centre, which was spotless, healthy and well fed. From the legal point of view it was a must. So our human body should be complete and untouched-to be master of a complete and healthy body is a spiritual act.

I am pained to state that you have not been keeping good health and a robust physique. Take this swing of health to a higher and healthier state of your body. Like a resolute recluse you must observe the stringest and hardest disciplines of life.

In this human world all rules, regulations and instructions become helpful if properly observed. Similarly regular yoga practice is quite useful. What is yoga? It is just to have full control over one's nerves, to regulate the circulation of one's blood in the whole body and to keep one's body-organs under one's complete control.

By observing these rules, you can keep this temple of God free, fit and healthy. This fragile human body can rise to the farthest heights of hilarity if its windows and doors are thrown open to let the light of God to enter in it. Keep on learning music regularly and learn it with zeal and vigour.

You may wonder that I am inspiring you to do physical exercise when I have not done the same in the whole of my life? Yes, my dear daughter, that is the primary reason why I am inspiring you for your physical-fitness. Had I practised regular physical exercise in my youth, I would have been a young, robust and healthy young man by now, radiating redness from my face. But I have become an old man whose body is withering and sitting at the eroding bank of this fast flowing life-river. I am living my life in acute pain and anguish.

I haven't done it
So you must do it.

There is nobody in this life who may love us selflessly. Everybody expects something in return for the love he professes for us. It is possible that you may give him in return your virtue, your beauty, sacrifice, good deeds or share with him your pangs of inner-love. So we only get what we give in return to our world. We must live our life in an examplary noble way so that we may get in return from the world maximum goodness, nobility and peace of mind. If the world does not give us anything in return for our good deeds and virtues, then we should fully understand that we had not lived a decent and virtuous life, had not fully friended our people and had not sacrificed our life in their service. Instead of cursing and finding faults with our parents, husbands, brothers, friends, relatives, children and acquaintances, we should search ourselves, peep within and declare that the world had not properly and nicely behaved with us, simply because we had not been fully true to ourselves. To curse ourselves for the sins of this world is the real moral and religious character. To search within the reasons for your inefficiency and defeat in life is the true religious character. Devoid of these qualities a man is not a human being but an animal.

There is nothing in our outer world that needs any special stress. Do not find excuses in other than yourself. That is the true renunciation and self-sacrifice. Those are the real aspects of religious truth or that truth that lies within us. The nicest thing of self knowledge is that we should forget yesterday of life for today and today for the coming morrow. We can get this message of forget and forgive in life from Omar Khayyam. His poetic philosophy is much near to this truth of life.

But the most important living pleasure is that we are in unison with God, who is within us. God, as expressed in different languages and various human thoughts, ultimately turns into a mythology. But when this truth is realized and revealed to a saintly person, it becomes his personal experience. No seeker of God believes in an impersonal God. Rather he realizes that God and myself are one and the same.

> Oh Nanak, have full faith in that Lord,
> Whose remembrance showers comforts and
>   absolves us from all miseries.

The moment we remember His name and realized His presence within us, we get purified through our inner-peace. I have explained to you how you can achieve Him. It is a blessing which gives you life and strength inwardly and enables you to know where to get it from. Now it is up to you to make efforts for achieving Him. The truth (a secret of God's knowledge) is to achieve self-realization. In addition to that whatever is there in Sikhism, it is of a secondary importance. Those who love other things more than God, are in fact dead objects.

My daughter, you kindle the life-fire in you and see to it that it turns into a flame. All virtues, all good deeds, all kinds of love, all sacrifices and self-devotion are there in life, so that we could rise above our physicality and sacrifice the maximum in us. If you discard this highest human virtue, simply to become noble and pure, then you are simply deceiving yourself. Our basic values-beauty, liking for His name and worship of God-have been taught to us by our loving Gurus and we must live our life in accordance to their teachings.

This gist of above is:-

(1) Everyday try to maximize this realization that your body is the temple of God.

(2) To realize that this body is the soul and it has to be pure and healthy in all respects.

(3) For your defeat and victory, hope and despair, fulfilment of desire and its remaining unfulfilled,

find reasons within yourself and not in others.

(4) Don't expect anything from others. Depend solely upon yourself. But give and distribute generously to others with a complete devotion to God.

(5) The world outside should touch you like the flowing water of a river just to enable you to have a bath. In this manner your soul will get purified and ennobled.

(6) Self-sacrifice and renunciation are only signs of a good character which a human being should perform for others. Beyond that there is nothing in them.

(7) Self-realization is our destination which we can achieve with the grace of Guru. This life is a struggle for self-understanding and we should not forget this basic fact. Inspite of having our houses built with jewels and pearls, Guru Nanak teaches us not to forget the Lord.

I think I have explained to you my view-point in a crystal clear manner and now I vehemently wish that Gargi should achieve her self-realization. The reasons for its success I try to find in myself and not in you. I bless you that you may live your life with full grace of God and feel happy in all sorts of circumstances.

I am-yours,
Puran Singh

Gwaliar-c.I
2-5-1923.

7. Suraiya (Gorakhpur)

From Simla, the son of Sir Sunder Singh Majithia came to Dehradun and suggested to Puran Singh to go to Suraiya Sugar Factory for guiding their children on Sikhism and for trying to grow Rosha grass on that land. This factory is situated at Sardar Nagar near Gorakhpur.

In 1924 he went to Sardar Nagar. Majithia's children gave him his due respect and were always at his service. All the servants were under the command of Puran Singh. Early in the morning a *Ragi* (Musician) used to recite *Asa Di Var* regularly. The whole family sat there for listening to this *Kirtan* (singing of hymns). Swamiji felt very happy and enjoyed the surroundings and atmosphere of the place very much. Day and night Puran Singh kept himself busy in studying chemistry books regarding the processing of sugar and in undertaking experiments with various chemicals. The sugar traders had promised that if he crystallized the processing of sugar without the use of bone charcoal (phosphorous) they would purchase the whole of the production at an enhanced rate. He was in a busy state of mind, constantly absorbed in thought as to how to achieve this desired objective. In that town of Sardar Nagar (Gorakhpur Dist.) there was neither any Chemistry laboratory nor any library of Chemistry journals, to guide him to the extent of uptodate research in this field in other countries. But Swami Puran Singh, by dint of his scientific knowledge and intuition was successful in inventing a new chemical by which the charcoal in bones was not used in crystalizing the processing of sugar. He got this invention patented under the trade mark of 'Rung Cup'. Afterwards when he returned to Dehradun, he by delving deep into the study of chemistry journals found that by his invention he had excelled the research in this field by 150 years. Mr. Gopal Rao, who at that time was a Chemist at the Forest Research Institute Dehradun was wonder-struck by his invention and that too without taking the help of any standard laboratory and library.

There was a big hospital in the premises of the factory, but when people came to know that Swamiji could properly diagnose their diseases and give medicine for curing them, many villagers started coming to him instead of going to the hospital.

Once when Swamiji advised a patient "Don't take *chapatti*, but can take rice." the answer he received was , " We are not fortunate enough to have born in a class which can enjoy rice."

This reply shocked Puran Singh. He realized that the cream of our food products was being consumed by our British rulers. It surprised him that those people had knowledge of food priorities attached to the privileged class. For a few days he went on repeating this. He used to say to the servent, "We are not born in that class that we should take other things. Bring waterfowl for me, order cake for me, cook zarda Pallao (a dish of rice). I am born in this class. I will not take anything except chicken. I am not born in any ordinary class of society. So saying he used to laugh and enjoy a great deal and used to crack jokes with others. But he did not cherish the treatment of a privileged class. He disliked the dandyism of rich men. He was always humane to the tenants and servants. Whenever there was a conflict or a quarrel, he always sided with the labourers.

He grew Rosha grass at Suraiya. Rosha grass is of two kinds-Motia and Sophia. From Motia Geranium oil can be distilled. But if Sophia oil and Motia are mixed up, it gives foulodour owing, to Sophia and does not fetch a good price. But it is very difficult to distinguish between Motia and Sophia. One can distinguish between the two when they have grown up to a height of about five feet.

Both kinds of grass grew in Suraiya. So to weed out Sophia grass, Swamiji would himself enter the muddy deep water. He went on with this exercise for several days and did not leave it to the servants as he feared that they might not take that much pains in extracting them out. But he asked them to pile up the Sophia grass plants in one place. And ultimately when he was satisfied that all the Sophia plants had been weeded out from the fields, he sprinkled sawdust, firewood and kerosene oil on it and set on it fire. Motia grass ultimately blossomed flowers and oil was distilled from it. This oil was later sold in the market to the Welcart Brothers.

In this way he was inventing many more things, for which experiments were in progress.

Suddenly one day he got enraged and became sick of Suraiya. For many days he remained inactive and idle. One evening he started singing:

This body was like a clog
On the ravine of Bliss-Spring,
Human vanity carried away by the flow of water
Has resulted into a wonderful gush of river water.
All discriminations of Duty, Debt and Need
Have flown into the wind.
Power and excesses have been ploughed down,
Turning it into a beautiful and smooth ploughed-
   field.
Through evil-eye and wrong methods
Clouds had gathered at the worldly door.
Behold, only one glance has
Wonderfully removed the whole headache.

When I heard him singing, I realized that his inner-self had become conscious and active. When I went to see him, he was severely weeping. Immediately he took paper, pen and inkpot and started writing down an essay in which he delineated the delicacy and purity of water, coupled with tender sentiments and appropriate similes. It was a lengthy essay and he named it Wagda Jal (Flowing water). He then called us, "Oh, Maya, Oh Biria, Oh Dad, come and listen to my `Flowing water',

He did not take much time to write down. Rather he was a very fast writer and he would never revise his first draft. Whatever has been written once, he would send it to the press for printing. When we saw and read the essay in print, we were wonderstruck to hear such a fine essay even in his disturbed state of mind. He had no personal agony in his mind, but could not tolerate injustice, excesses and cruelties inflicted on others. Without caring for his personal losses, he used to quarrel with those who had such barbaric feelings, because his injured sensitivity could not tolerate ill-treatment of others.

8. Sheikhupura

It was Swamiji's belief that nothing perishes in this world. So any loss was never a loss to him. This, one can easily judge from one fact. In the Bar forests in district Sheikhupura, sixteen squares of land was sanctioned in his favour. The number of our *chak* (area) was 73/19 in which totally *vann* trees had grown. It was such a thick forest that the rays of the sun could not penetrate it to touch the earth. All the sixteen squares were covered with *vann* trees. There were about a hundred wells in that area. Since the ground water-level was very high, seepage seemed to have affected the area and that poor quality land was allotted to him. Many people advised Swamiji to go there and verify the quality of the land. But he replied, "Has anybody ever checked the teeth of a gifted-horse?". When another man said, "But we properly test a pitcher worth four annas before purchasing it." He said, "One should have these tests before purchasig it, but I am not purchasing anything. It is a gift. Another person retorted, "Sometimes a free gift turns out to be a white elephant." But he did not listen to anybody's advice and went to Delhi to enter into an agreement with the government. He also employed a *munshi* (Clerk) for the job and instructed him to start the wood-cutting. The *munshi* went to the site to inspect the area where *vann* trees had grown in such large numbers that even the rays of the sun could not peep in. The clerk returned with the suggestion that the Jat farmers of the area were prepared to do the wood-cutting themselves and were also ready to purchase all the wood. Without listening to anything, he scolded him, "Look, are you an employee of a businessman? It is a royal land and cannot be entrusted to any Tom, Dick or Harry." The *munshi* said, "Where shall we store the wood? It is better to auction it." He scolded him, "Go away. First of all you auction me and then my wood. You allow all of them to take as much wood as they can carry."

The clerk went back to Sheikhupura where people were anxiously awaiting to purchase the wood. But the clerk announced the orders of Sardar Sahib saying, "The wood of royal squares will never be auctioned. It will be better to burn it. You can take as much as you like." They all appreciated his generosity with one voice, "wonderful, we have never seen such a generous a person in our life."

They all became eager to see him. The trees were being felled and men, women, boys, girls – all carried away the wood without any hinderance.

When Gian Chand Chopra, who was a rich man came to know of it he thought that he too would reap a profit out of if and it would not be difficult to make such a philanthropist agree. Swamiji agreed to allow him to plough and grow cotton on that land for two years. He came all the way to Dehradun, purchased some fruits and flower garlands for Swamiji and came to our bungalow 'Iven'. At that time Swamiji was strolling in the garden. After confirming his identity from the servants, he fell on Swamiji's feet. He said, "I have come to have your darshan (glimpse) for I have heard a great deal about you that you are a real faqir (recluse). I also want your solution for my mental misgivings." Swamiji started sermonising him to help in getting him rid of his mental problems. He took tea and lunch with us and also slept for sometime at our place. At the time of the evening tea, he said, "Sir, I have another request to make to you. I had visited your land and your clerk was not discharging his duties properly. If you kindly permit me to grow cotton on your land for two years, I will manage the Wood-cutting and ploughing of the entire land." To this Swamiji replied,"My agreement with the government is to grow 'Rosha grass'". He said, "alright sir, after getting the entire area ploughed I will grow Rosha grass and cotton both." But he was, somehow, able to convince Swamiji to grow cotton as well as Rosha grass in the field. But he got the land ploughed and started growing only cotton. He bribed our clerks so that they did not report to us. Other inhabitants of the locality were surprised to find that Swamiji did not come even once to see his land. They were jealous of Gian Chand and said, "Hats off to Sardar Sahib. We were prepared to pay him the price, but he did not agree and this karar (kshetri) has taken charge of the entire land without paying him anything."

Gian Chand sold out his entire cotton crop for the first year and for the second year he had also made arrangements for the sale of most of his crop. But this time he did not seem to have sufficiently bribed our clerk. Our clerk reached Dehradun and complained , "Sir, he hasn't grown a single plant of the grass. The entire grass-seeds packed in bags are rotting and being wasted ." Swamiji was astounded. He immediately ordered the clerk to go back immediately and turn out Gian Chand forthwith. "It is a governmental order to grow the Rosha grass on that land. He has gone against his words. Don't allow him to touch anything," He said. Poor Gian Chand had to leave a portion of his cotton-crop standing on the field and leave the place immediately.

Till the end of 1925 Swamiji did not pay even a single visit to his land. People often remarked about his perseverance. When Swamiji visited it for the first time in 1926, he found that some people had planted wheat, cotton and maize on it. In fact the entire land was being utilized for these crops alone. When he saw that his orders had been completely disobeyed, he grew enraged and got the whole land ploughed for growing Rosha grass. In 1928 Rosha grass grew to its full hight for the first time. It had grown as high as five feet and with the blowing of breeze, it used to embrace each other. Swamiji enjoyed this scene with the aid of his telescope, sitting on the first floor of the house. It made him extremely happy and was always calculating the quantum that he would be getting out of it. But by the will of God, there were floods all around with five feet deep water in the house, grass-fields and the factory. He had got prepared a grating frame for filling grass in it with the help of stilts. He climbed on the top of it with a box full of his manuscripts. There was water everywhere.

He had asked his servants to shift to safer places in other squares. This seclusion added to his blissful temperament and he started to dance and sing.

> Thank God, my spinning wheel has been reduced
>   to pieces,
> And it has absolved me of all my miseries.

When he was singing this couplet, many people from adjoining squares came on camel backs to rescue the stranded Swamiji. But they found that Swamiji, drenched with pleasure and delight, continued singing the same song over and over again.

When they entreated him to come down and take shelter in their house he replied, 'Whose house is this?" and again started singing:

Recognize Him in all things, situations and ways of life.
If you are a lover, recognize your beloved in every colour.
Don't consider Him alone and lonely,
Search Him in your narrow heart,
Recognize Him in every garden, street and company.

Seeing him intoxicated with pleasure in spite of this huge loss all of them were wonder-struck. They went back to their houses uttering, "Oh, God." "Oh, God". At night in the light of the full moon the entire sky became clear. The flood-water had also started receding. All the servants came back to him. He also came down and went up to his first floor room singing this couplet.

If you are a lover, recognize your beloved in every colour.

People living at that place considered him to be a saint. When he came back to Dehradun, he told me the whole story, "Look Maya, people of the area are just fools. They are not aware of the fact that the flood-waters have provided so much manure to the Rosha grass, which I otherwise could not provide them. I was dancing under the intoxication of this delight:

If you are a lover, recognize your beloved in every colour.

Swamiji wrote his autobiography in 1927 at square No.73/19, in which he mentioned the detailed activities of the revolutionaries and his meeting with Khudadad who was a real genius. But in a fit of ill-temper he burnt it down. Many more manuscripts had met their end in this way.

People of the area used to throng to our place in large numbers. Swamiji met them without any reservation. Here Swamiji found a new lease of life. His eyes got back the same glint of intoxication of pleasure which he had previously experienced in 1912. Drenched in delight, he used to sing this song which was his maiden one:

Father and son or friend and foe,
Lover and beloved, none is our's
It is a strange deliverance,
Neither we belong to anyone

Nor any one belongs to us.
No seeker is our's
We have also not desired anyone ardently.
We haven't enjoyed the waves of pleasure,
And haven't moaned for pain or misery.
Neither we have sown nor reaped the crop,
We haven't ploughed or thrashed the field.
The moment the veil of fallacy vanished,
Oh, we felt intoxicated with pleasure.
It is only the thing of the past,
When one was my pal and other a stranger.
Someone was my grand-daughter or grandson,
Or I was paternal and maternal grandfather
Preserved cereal with one and pestled with another,
Grinded it hither and sifted it thither.
The moment my heart was relieved from the cluster of fallacies.
Only then the revelation came to me.
There was a time when we had a big shop
At one time we had a big profession,
Sycophancy at one place and welcome at another
Service with one and respect for the other,
Belonging to high caste or possessor of attributions
Boasting of position and pride of family
With the vanishing of ego, I beheld
There was neither position nor family
I was itching for a fight with someone,
And falling at the feet of another,
Riots with someone for my rights
And have an unjustified fight with the other.
Just now this whim dominated me,
Scold some-one and quarrel with another.
The moment duality vanished in me, I was wonder-struck
Where to fight, whom to fight?

    The children of the forest-inhabitants flocked to him for listening to his songs. They heard and observed his each gesture attentively, because they had never seen anybody so strange and saintly in their life. The women folk of the area also used to say in appreciation, "His clerk was perfectly right in calling him a king. The poet in him was in fact, giving vent to his blissful feelings and was expressing his concern for all living-beings. With tears in his eyes, he used to glance on all sides and sing:

> I find you everywhere, all over,
> Not that I yearn to have a glimpse of you,
> Not that I am in quest of you,
> 'Oh dazzling power, your beauty is stunning,
> And I feel your presence every moment of my life.

He enjoyed his free-life here. There were neither houses nor high buildings. When he saw young grazier-girls and young herdboys looking after their grazing herds, he used to lift the passing young goats and enjoy embracing them. The elderly people had to look aside to hide their smile but the children openly laughed to their heart's content. Sometimes they encircled him.

Swamiji used to dance while embracing these young children. People enjoyed such hilarious scenes and some even composed poetry on it:

> Oh! my spinning wheel, revolve,
> Your supports are made of cane.
> Guests, who have visited us,
> Belong to very far-off places.
> Their eyes are like flamebeams,
> Worth preserving for ever and for life.

Just as the bee gathers the honey, so Swamiji also concentrated his diffused emotions and started singing, looking deep into their eyes:

> Neither you exist now, nor I am anywhere,
> Forgetfulness prevails everywhere.

He injected his bliss to the person he embraced making him feel jubilant with joy. He glanced deeply at known or unknown people alike and thoroughly understood them. He embraced standing trees and climbing plants as though they were his long separated kith and kin.

Taking off his shirt he used to often lie down on the Rosha grass and graze the grass like animals.

Once Dr. Balbir Singh visited the area. Swamiji took him to the fields where Rosha grass, in their prime youth, were dancing to the tune of the singing breeze. Swamiji took off his shirt, lay down on it and gently embraced the grass. And Dr. Balbir Singh could not resist his temptation of doing the same.

When the sun first rose in the sky each morning he used to open his mouth to drink the whole of its redness and then started singing:

> I drink the light every moment,
> Filling my peg with intoxicant,
> The sky is like my measure
> Filled to the brim with the wine of light.

At the time of sunset, the redness scattered around the sun, bewitched him very much and he started wrapping it around his body, as if he wanted to absorb the whole of it. At the time of sunset, a special bewitching redness radiates from the sun. One day when I saw him drenched in its beauty, I asked him,"What are you dong?" "I am trying to preserve this gold-laced veil of the sun. Why do you disturb me? Better enjoy it for yourself, see thither." Then he started singing:

> Your bewitching eyes have sent me a love-hint,
> Enjoying it fully, my eyes have instantly responded,
> Fountains of affection sprang from your eyes.
> My eyes felt soothed and drank it to their fill.

He was a believer of unity and an amorist who could extract pleasure out of everything.

When he became completely intuned with nature, he used to say, "Maya, I am feeling complete solace and tranquility."

Sitting on the first floor, Swamiji with his telescope could easily spot any person passing through his land and would instruct his clerk to go and fetch him. There was a thoroughfare beside our plot which led to a near by village. So people kept on passing through that way. One day a man on camel-back, was passing by. Swamiji commanded his clerk to run and catch him. The clerk brought him to Swamiji. Now this passer-by was the owner of one hundred squares of land. Feeling annoyed, he said, "Oh Sardara, with great difficulty and hardship, you have become an owner of just sixteen squares of land. This much area I have left for the grazing of my animals."

Swamiji replied, "Your hundred squares are not giving that much returns as mine. Moreover, I am not the owner of these squares. It is government property. I have grown that valuable grass which was not possible to grow in this area. The government has specially sanctioned an opening of the canal for it. If this grass gets crushed under your camel's feet, it will be a great loss to me."

The camel rider said, "May God bless you. But please don't create difficulties for the people."

To this Swamiji replied, "I will get a special passage made for people to pass conveniently." Gladdened with pleasure and filling his eyes with tears of delight the camel rider remarked, " May God bestow upon you a long and prosperous life. Your kingdom may last for ever. You are exactly of the same generous temperament as I had heard of you."

It is impossible to fully pen down his nature and temperament. When we try to capture his open nature with the help of sordid words, it gets concretised and changed. With the help of minute sensitivity and rich experience, it is just like capturing the sudden flash of the lightning. He was in unison with the whole cosmos and had an extraordinary capability and intuition. He was able to control all this superb powers within the fold and embrace of his two arms. Only that person could stay and live with him who had full control over his body, mind and views. Wherever he lived and in whatever state of mind he was passing through, he had the capability and capacity of keeping his routes intact and could easily extract his spiritual food for his soul.

Whenever the Deputy Commissioner came to inspect the area, he used to stay at the Rest House which was about two miles from our farm. One day when Swamiji went to see him he was told that he was sleeping. But he went straight to his room and said, "Gentleman, have you come here for taking rest or for listening to the grievances of the public and for taking a decision?" He immediately got up and started asking his opinion about all the distinguished persons of the area. His reply was "You have mistaken me. I am not from the C.I.D. department." Hearing this reply the Deputy Commissioner kept mum. When Swamiji came out of the room, everybody was wondering about his guts; how daringly he had entered the Deputy Commissioner's room. For the people of the area, Deputy Commissioner was more powerful than God.

Similarly he did not spare the police-station in charge, the Tahsildar, the *Patwari* (village registrar) or any other important government official. One of our servants Sham Singh narrated to us an intereting incident. One day the *Patwari* had come to see him. Swamiji called Sham Singh aloud, "Oh, Sham Singh, Oh Sham Singh."

"Yes sir," replied the servant.

"Beat shoes on the *Patwari's* head; he misbehaves and tortures the poor people." Sham Singh fully realized that Swamiji was enraged. He immediately brought him a glass of water and a hand-fan. After he had the water he immediately calmed down.

If the police-station in charge ever visited the area, Swamiji used to say, " Is there any one here whom you suspect? Please go away, I have no time for every Tom, Dick or Harry. Only bread-earners live here and you suspect them to be thieves? Who will work for us? My servants are busy in their work the whole day and they cannot spare even a single moment for committing a theft." He used to return with a blank face.Not a single person was arrested by the police till he was there. In fact, the people living there did not commit any theft. The people living in that forest area used to say, "Sardarji has taken our responsibility. We will not let him down."

These forest-inhabitants bore a good moral character. After the battle of Alexander and Porus, some of the soldiers who had accompanied Alexander had decided to settle down here. These people were descendants of them. They had camels, a very strong sturdy animal which could travel hundred of miles overnight. They used to commit theft with the help of their camels and to destroy all evidence of their footprints, they used to keep quilts under their camel's feet. Day by day the number of thefts started increasing. To provide them with adequate work, the government took up the consolidation of holdings.

The inhabitants of these forests have a very long height and their children resemble Europeans in colour and features. They have a very high sense of morality and strictly stand by their promises and commitments. They always have fair-dealings with each other. Truthful by nature they did not bear malice against anyone nor betray any one. They treated us very nicely.

Swamiji used to embrace or hug them and walk with them with arm-in-arm. These gestures pleased them very much and they often discussed it among themselves. The man who cares a fig for the Deputy Commissioner and is an awe even for the police, embraces us and walks with us arm-in-arm.

Whenever he was immensely pleased and overjoyed, he used to keep baskets full of sweetmeats in the open courtyard and ask them to loot it. Someone would be successful in taking a larger quantity than others and then they would start quarrelling amongst themselves. Swamiji always sided with the person who had taken a larger quantity because, according to hir it was the sign of his bravery and briskness.

He always enjoyed a quarrel whether between elders or children. Their taunts and sarcasms to each other revealed their inner feelings.

Once Swamiji had given a big piece of ice to a little girl. But her mother instructed her to keep it safe till all family members returned from work. It is the habit of these forest dwellers to share whatever they eat. Even if it is one apple and the family members are fifteen, they will share it among themselves. So, the little girl put away the whole piece of ice in a pot and busied herself in play. When all family members returned home from the field they asked the girl to bring that novelty which Sardarji had given her. But alas when the girl went to fetch it she was baffled and mystified to find nothing in the pot.

When her mother ordered her daughter to come out in the courtyard and asked, "Where is that novelty which Sardar had given you?" She innocently replied, "I had kept it in the pot, but now there is nothing." Her mother beat her severely and scolded her saying, "You have followed the habits of these city-dwellers. You must have consumed the whole of it and are now telling a lie."

The girl bitterly wept and cried aloud, "Sardarji, rescue me from this beating."

Swamiji was at that time sitting in his first floor room writing. Hearing all the commotion he came down and saw that all family-members were abusing and scolding the girl for having allegedly consumed that novelty all by herself. In the beginning Swamiji could not fully understand the whole situation. But when he realised what it was all about he explained to them that it was not a piece of sweetmeat he had given but a piece of ice which had melted. But they did not believe his explanation because they had never seen ice before and did not know that it melts. Swamiji asked his servant to bring another piece of ice from his room. He gave that piece of ice to one girl Bego by name and instructed her to hold it tightly in her hand. After a couple of minutes the girl cried out, "I cannot hold it any longer, my hand is getting benumbed." He asked them to bring a pot and instructed Bego to put that piece of ice in it. "now keep a strict watch on it and see how it melts into water." Swamiji cautioned her.

After some time that piece of ice melted into water. Seeing this mystery performed before her very eyes. Bego said, "as you city-dwellers can easily break your promises, so are your deceptive things."

The morality of these forest-inhabitants was exemplary and worth praising.

We had separate opening of water sanctioned in our name. But someone disturbed that opening and started the draining of the water to his fields. He was unknown to Swamiji. When someone else noticed this illegal action, he cautioned him, "What the hell have you done? You are not fully aware of Sardarji's temperament. He will haul you up and hang you." The defaulter was so such terrified that he immediately brought a white-piece of cloth and threw that cloth on the head of my grand-daughter (Gargi's daughter) who was playing in the courtyard. Swamiji was already enraged and the presence of the defaulter in his courtyard further increased the intensity of his anger. Another forest inhabitant standing close by said, "Now you cannot harm or punish him because he has come to take your shelter. We forest-dwellers have a social custom. Generally nobody will put white cloth on the opponent's head because we are revengeful people and it is customary for us either to avenge or to redeem. Now that he has has brought this white cloth here, it indicates that he has surrendered himself to you and is seeking your shelter. If someone does not accept this apology or surrender, he is socially boycotted. You may kindly pardon him and shake hands with him as a gesture of forgiveness."

So long as we remained in that area, that man and all the members of his family remained obedient to us. They were very eager to be of some service to Sardarji. One day his son came to me and said, "Sardarniji, we are prepared to behead any enemy of Sardarji, wherever he may be". I cautioned him not to say this to Swamiji because he had enmity with none. Haven't you heard him singing.

"Neither I have any enemy
Nor any friend is mine."

If we got more work from a labourer by praising him or tempting him with a gift, he would always disapprove of it and even scold us. "Your temptation of a gift was like an intoxicant which prompted him to forget his fatigue." He was very kind and generous to the labourers. At times he would give to them all the money that he had in his pocket at that moment. He was very much concerned about the dress and diet of the labourers and wanted it to be as nice as those of his own. If any labourer expressed some liking for any utensil or any cloth, he would immediately hand it over to him with pleasure. He had deep love for diligent bread earners. Whenever he found any one down with fatigue, he would immediately advise him to go and take complete rest. How could these labourers ever expect any maltreatemet from a generous and kind-hearted person like Swamiji?

At the Rosha grass farm, Swamiji had issued specific instructions to all, not to prepare cowdung cakes or burn these, because its manure was very useful for Rosha grass. They were allowed to use as much fire-wood as they needed. One day he went deep into the farm lands and was shocked to see cowdung cakes stuck on a wall. All grown up family members had gone for reaping the crops except the children. When the children saw Sardarji coming, they were overjoyed and brought out a cot for him to rest. But Swamiji had become an embodiment of anger and disgust. He ordered those innocent and carefree children to take the cot inside saying, "You are burning my gold!"

His clerk always accompanied him wherever he went. He ordered him to put up 'offenders' accounts before him which he immediately finalized. For about three hours he restlessly waited for the others to come. Sometimes he would sit under the shade of the tree and at others he used to pace about. But his attention was focussed on the road waiting for their return. He had made up his mind to ask them to leave the place.

When all the family members returned from reaping with sickles in their hands, their faces reddened due to the scorching heat of the sun, dust spread all over their faces, and sweatdrops beautifying them as dew-drops on the roses he forgot everything and embraced them saying, "Oh, my real bread earners. I am getting everything because of you." They innocently asked him, "Sardarji, how is it that you have come here in this heat ?"

Swamiji forgot everything and happily returned home, which was at a sufficient distance. Entering his house, he said, "Maya, today I have enjoyed roaming amidst roses".

His clerk had narrated the whole incident to us later on. After hearing that Swamiji had been enraged by noticing the prepared cowdung cakes I reminded Sardarji, "If cowdung cakes had not been there, how could you have composed such a wonderful poem 'Ahiran Gohe Thapdi' (An Ahiran girl preparing cowdung cakes). Hearing this he laughed very much.

There was a time when he was not prepared to marry me, but afterwards he developed such an intimate attachment for me as he was not prepared to live alone. Whatever he wrote, he used to read it out to me. In spite of the fact that I was totally illiterate, he used to ask my approval. Whatever did not appeal to me, he used to cross it out, saying, "I don't lose anything by crossing it out." One day somebody was sitting with us. When Swamiji asked my opinion about one of his writings, that man remarked, "What does she know about literature?"

"No, she is my source of inspiration and experience. That is the reason why I do not allow her to go anywhere without me." said Swamiji.

Whenever my mother sent me a message to come and meet her, he used to allow me to go to her but on the condition that I should daily write to him or send a telegram. Once I went to Kohmarri (Marri hills). I instructed my brother Bhakat Sain Dass to wire Swamiji regarding my safe arrival. He, being a man of old values did not realise the gravity and significance of the situation and did not send him a telegram.

When he did not hear anything from my side, Swamiji started speculating, "Had Maya been alive, she must have sent me a telegram. Possibly, she may be dead and those foolish people may cremate her without my presence. What shall I do in that case?" When such apprehensions overpowered him, he boarded a train for Kohmarri without taking his leave. When he reached Kohmarri, he saw us taking our meals. Finding me there he started weeping and said, "Thank God, you are alive. I was under the fear that you might be dead and they might have cremated you by this time without informing me. Why didn't you wire me about your safe arrival?"

Completely perplexed, I could not utter a single word.

He commanded, "Alright, now you get ready, as we are to leave this place immediately. I have come here without taking leave."

My mother started weeping bitterly and in between it, she asked me, "Maya are you going?"

Inspite of fully realizing my mother's misery and agony I had no other alternative but to say, "Yes".

My mother, deeply touched and agonised, threatened me, "If you go now, I will never call you in future."

Leaving my meals half way through I accompanied him. At the time of my leaving, I was also weeping bitterly.

On the way to Dehradun, he tried to pacify me saying, "I know you are weeping for the apprehension that your mother might never call you in future. Mothers can never be so cruel and harsh. You are married to an ascetic who has always told you:

> Father and son, or friend and foe,
> Lover and beloved, none is our's,
> It is a strange deliverance,
> Neither we belong to any one,
> Nor anyone else belongs to us.

Hearing this I stopped weeping.

Whenever I went to Kohmarri, he would start wiring me from the very first day of my arrival, to finalize my programme of prompt returning to Dehradun. His telegrams were not short, but ran into fifty or sixty words. People used to say, "Bhakatji's sister has come here, no doubt, but she has never stayed here even for ten days at a stretch after her marriage." But whenever he accompanied me to my parent's house, we stayed for a much longer period. Once we went together to my niece's marriage. Our entire family-members had gathered on the ground floor for singing songs. He asked me not to go to the ground floor, but I insisted.

"No" he persisted.

"Yes, I must go". I replied in a determined voice.

After sometime I went down to participate in the singing of songs. When everybody had left for their homes, I came up and quietly went to my bed. In the adjoining room the son-in-law of my cousin was putting up. In the morning he tauntingly asked me, "At night, there was lot of 'No' and 'Yes'" I replied, "We are not like you."

He translated Tolstoy's *Resurrection* into Punjabi and titled it *Moyan Di Jaag*. He took just eighteen days to complete the translation of this huge work. This rendering was done at Sheikhupura at our farm-land, where we all were living. The table where he used to work, was always swinging on one way or the other. Even the light of the earthen lamp was not sufficient. He enjoyed reading and writing so much, that he never felt tired in this exercise. After completing its translation, he quietly put it in my lap. I did not express any sign of pleasure, as I apprehended that my expression of delight over the completion of this work might not tempt him to start another. But even till today I feel guilty for not expressing at that moment, my pleasure and satisfaction for the completion of this monumental work.

One day while reciting 'Sukhmani' (The Pslam of Peace), he forgot some lines repeatedly. So he resolved to learn the whole of it by heart. Whole of the day he kept on cramming it. When he was satisfied that he had learnt it by heart he asked me to take his test. From whichever portion I asked him to repeat , he was able to recite the same quite accurately. Then he said, "Now please listen to the whole of 'Sukhmani' . He was able to recite accurately the whole of it in such a fast speed that he finished it within half-an-hour.

He neither used any dictionary nor had studied any book on prosody. According to him only those persons used dictionaries or books on prosody who were hollow and their words did not carry any grit. He never derived any inspiration from any one. Whenever he sat down to write anything, it seemed as though he was just looking at the thing minutely clasping it. The sheer enjoying of it delighted him and his mind was fully occupied. No other thought could enter his mind to disturb him. He was, in fact, a sky artist who could fly to the farthest heights, writing his compositions. At that moment he had very little contact with the earth. His way of doing work or expressing love were strange and distinct. Whatever he performed, he used his spiritual power for it.

If somebody disturbed him while he was busy writing he felt so perturbed and dejected, as if he had fallen from the farthest heights and broken into pieces. So everybody kept mum and remained silent at the time of his writing. *Sisters of the Spining Wheel* (in English) was completed wthin eight days. He devoted all those days and nights in writing it and did not come out of his room till it was completed. The servants used to quietly leave water, tea, and a few eatables for him. If he felt like taking anything, he consumed them otherwise those things remained untouched. None of us went to his room, as our presence could disturb him. When he came out with his complete manuscript after eight days, he asked Dr. Khudadad to stretch out his hand. He had hidden his manuscript in his hands at the back. After receiving it, Khudadad remarked, "Some books are worth their diamonds, others in gold and still others in pearls, but this book is of albumen-worth. *Sisters of the Spinning Wheel* was printed abroad in 1921 and its introduction was written by Arnest Ridge.

Sardar Sampuran Singh Barrister was at that time living at Lyalpur. He had great affection and regards for Swamiji. His whole family loved and held Swamiji in great esteem, as if he were a member of their own family. Swamiji did not bother about formalities such as,"please" or "kindly". If some body ever said, "Please take this *parshad*", he would retort immediately, "Being animals, why do you use the word *parshad* " He used the word 'manger' for meals. Whenever he visited Sardar Sampuran Singh he used to call aloud from outside. "Oh sister, what is ready in the manger?" The reply he used to get was, "Brother, it is what domestic animals eat."

"But sister, are you aware that sometimes lions also accompany domestic animals?"

She fully understood that by it he meant that her brother wanted to enjoy chicken. So she used to reply, "The lion will have to wait for his food." But lions know no waiting." he would say. He used to talk in this informal way.

If he made up his mind about something, he was determined to achieve it ! Our post-office was at Sayyad Wale. He had deputed one servant especially for bringing his daily mail from the post-office. Often when he had left for the post-office, Swamiji thought of posting some more letters. So another person was sent. Sometimes it so happened that in a day three to four persons had to run to the post-office. And so he thought of requesting the postal authorities to open a new post-office in that place. On enquiring, he was told that for it a substantial quantum of mail had to be received everyday. For getting a temporary post-office opened, he asked many booksellers to send him books through V.P. He also sent self-addressed envelopes to his acquaintances to post him letters. He instructed all the inhabitants of the surrounding villages to receive letters at his address and distributed to them many stamped envelopes free of cost. *Very shortly a post office* was opened there.

Similarly he felt that there should be a cattledetainment house in the area because many stray buffaloes grazed and spoiled his grass. To get it going, he used to send his own cattle to the detainment house. Whenever he saw his own cattles wandering he used to order his servants to take them to the cattle-detainment house. His tenants used to say in an appreciative tone, "His temperament and generosity are those of a king." Eventually a permanent cattle-detainment house was sanctioned for the area.

The Marriage of His Daughter

It was decided to celebrate the marriage of Gargi at Rawalpindi in February 1928. As he had never attended any ceremony connected with such occasions he had no knowledge of them. Whenever he went to Rawalpindi, people used to flock to him to listen to his inspiring and instructive discourses for overcoming their agonies and miseries of life. This continued for as long as he was at Rawalpindi. We reached Rawalpindi well in advance and rented a huge building belonging to Sardar Buta Singh. People felt doubly rejoiced - one for the marriage and the other for Swamiji's presence. Since it was a marriage celebration, singing of folk songs and other entertainments continued until late at night. He used to sit amongst the gathered people and enjoy it all. The hall could accommodate about two hundred and fifty persons. The celebrations continued for some days. Now it was time to distribute *bhaji* (sweetmeats) among all friends and relatives. But some of the relatives refused to accept it. The father-in-law of the girl's uncle and father-in-law of the boy's brother who had decided not to participate in this marrige-celebration refused to accept our bhaji, with the resutl that many families directly related to them also refused to attend the marriage. In the beginning these bickerings did not come out openly. We failed to comprehend the complexities of these vexed problems. When the marriage day was very near, Swamiji came to know of these family bickerings and non-acceptance of *bhaji*. He became furious. I was watching the setting arrangements of the girl's clothes to be given in the dowry. He called me aloud, "Maya - come down." I immediately came down. He roared in anger, "throw everything here and pack your luggage for going back to Dehradun".

Witnessing the working of this world, he had fully realized that whatever was happening. was destined to happen. No use in criticising it. At the time of such huge celebration in which one's mind felt fully absorbed, sometimes a glitter of indecisiveness was witnessed in such a way that one's mind did not become resolute and firm.

First of all the large scale celebrations had been organised for fully rejoicing that happy occasion. There were no limits to ardent desires and intrinsic pleasures. The celebrations were being conducted in proper and congenial conditions. We had not the slightest apprehension of any unfortunate and untoward happening.

I started the packing of my luggage thinking all the while "Probably it was all because of me, so that I did not forget myself in the celebrations of those worldly - pleasures." I considered that whole incident as destined and pregnant with mystic meaning.

Swamiji declared, "I am not going to marry my daughter in such a mean family."

Hearing this, all relatives got together. Gargi was weeping. Swamiji consoled her, "Why are you weeping? I will get you married to a much better person with all pomp and show." Before long these very relatives ran to our place and fell on his feet. "We are prepared to honour your *bhaji* even if you present them in shoes. Please don't do this. Such incidents had never happened since the days of Adam and Eve."

"But it will happen now. I will do it" Swamiji said in a very determined voice.

Somebody said, "You have bought so much of provisions. What will you do with them?"

"I will distribute them among the poor", he replied.

We got ready for leaving the place. The bridegroom (Malik Amar Singh) was shocked when be learnt everything. He sought permission to meet Swamiji. But Swamiji told the messanger to convey to him, "I don't want to meet any person from this mean family. My daughter cannot live with such narrow-minded people. "I will arrange her marriage somewhere else."

The bridegroom again sent a message, "I want to see Puran Singh the poet." I don't know in what manner it was conveyed to him, but it did soften Puran Singh. The bridegroom came there without permission and the poet Puran Singh welcomed him with an embrace. But Amar Singh Malik was weeping bitterly. He pacified him and embracing him tightly he started singing:

SHEIKHUPURA

> Ascetic, thou art God himself
> Thou the bridegroom, thou art bride,
> Thou the father, thou the mother,
> Thou the Ranjha
> Thou the Heer,
> Forget not your Heer
> Weep not in the wilderness
> None, here, there or anywhere,
> Compares with thou.
> Even in taunt, sarcasm or service
> Thou can find—your Heer.
> Oh ascetic, thou art God.

Everybody felt relieved that a very wise decision had been taken. The feeling of disunity amongst us immediately vanished like mist. Everybody started laughing, singing and dancing again Drenched in ecstasy and blossomed with happiness, Swamiji got up and requested the girls already singing, to vacate the arena for him. He started singing loud:

> Congratulations for the blossomed disposition
> This state of juicy fragrance is Jamshed's measure itself
> Even the moon is paying his felicitous obeisance
> The bend in his waist, clearly shows it
> Drink and drink in uncounting measures
> Drench yourself with innumerable measures
> Your's is the hegemony over millions and millions.

So days passed by in enjoyment. Very soon Bhai Sudh Singh *Ragi* (musician) with his companions arrived there and created a new type of atmosphere. *Rahras* was recited in the evening followed by recitation of bani (hymns) with the help of musical instruments. Early in the morning *Asa Di Var* was recited and many people gathered there for enjoying it.

At night Bhai Sudh Singh said, "Kindly make arrangements for hot water for our morning baths." Swamiji replied, "First have your inner baths and then the outer." Bhai Sudh Singh thought that Swamiji was perhaps in a mood to give a discourse on self-purification. So he said, "How can that be achieved?" Swamiji retorted, "Are you ignorant of that? First take tea in the morning." All the musicians laughed but some misgivings seemed to have remained unresolved in their minds.

They asked somebody for clarification of his statement. "We are still at a loss to know why and for what Puran Singh had made that statement." He explained, " It is not so easy to grasp the statements of Puran Singh in their entirety. But whatever he states it is always true."

The marriage procession arrived and later at night everybody retired to their beds after taking their dinner. There was a special arrangement for the recitation of *Asa Di Var* in the morning. The hall where the Guru Granth Sahib *(Adi Granth)* was kept, was decorated in a regal manner. Costly head-scarfs laced with gold and silver glittered everywhere. Everybody was sitting in reverence to the *Adi Granth*. Swami Narain, who was a dear disciple of Ram Tirath, had also come, He was also enjoying the celebrations. When the recitation of *Asa Di Var* came to its completion, the bride and the bridegroom, were seated in front of the *Adi Granth*. Puran Singh was already occupyin the exalted seat very near to the *Adi Granth*. Tears were dripping out of Puran Singh's eyes. He opened his eyes and said, "The marriage ceremony is complete and there is no need for *lawan phere* (going around the *Adi Granth*)". Every body was stunned to hear it especialy the bride who seemed very much perplexed. For sometime there was complete silence. Then he said, "You all are slaves of ceremonies, do as you like." The bridegroom and the bride went around the *Adi Granth* four times and thus the *lawan phere* were completed.

In the evening it was time to say good-bye to the bride. The scullions came with a palanquin. Both the palanquin and its scullions looked very shabby. Seeing the shabby condition of the palanquin he said, "What is this nonsense? Who dares to take my darling daughter in this rotten palanquin?" He roared in such a way that everybody was terrified and puzzled. "Take away this rotten one. My daughter will not step into this shabby palanquin. Leave the place immediately", he ordered. The terrified scullions promptly went away with the palanquin. Everybody present there failed to understand the situation and started whispering to each other, "You can't depend on this father, he may order his daughter to come out even after stepping into the palanquin." Bibi Attar Kaur came running to the place. Fully realizing the gravity of the situation, she recollected that the Sardar family had recently got a new palanquin ready. And so, she somehow managed to get this new, decorated and sparkling palanquin. It had a gold-laced cover-cloth over it. The marriage-custom is that the parents lift the bride for seating her in the palanquin. But he said, "Gargi, get up and be seated in the palanquin." Gargi started weeping and this scene of departure, prompted others to shed tears. He said, "Please stop weeping. If I started weeping, no body will be able to stop me from it." Gargi stepped in the palanquin. He did not allow any one else to touch her palanquin except Dr. Balbir Singh, Dr. Khudadad, Bhakat Sain Dass(bride's maternal uncle) and himself. All the four lifted the palanquin on their shoulders and hastened towards Gargi's in-laws house. People kept on saying, "Please stop, please stop" but they promptly reached their destination (Malik Amar Singh's house). Men and women could not keep up with their fast-pace. After leaving Gargi in her in - law's house, he left for his farm-land (Sheikhupura) in the evening along with his guests who had come from that place.

His heart was drenched in grief at parting with his daughter. The memory of parting with his daughter was still afresh and disturbing him. At his farm-land he seemed to find everybody engulfed in a similar grief and agony. He felt as though all animals were drinking nothing else but grief and misery. He enquired of them:

> No one understands your anguish and agony
> Concealed in your trembling voice of Ku hu
> Oh dove, with such beautiful and attractive attire,
> Why are you so sad and gloomy?
> Your silent activity in managing your livelihood,
> Your defeat like tolerance in braving your miseries
>   without any protest,
> It is no way less than the renunciation of a real
>   saint.
> In your sweet moving voice,
> Is hidden your saddest and purest agony
> Which in fact, is an attractive beauty.

Saturated with intense feelings, he went on composing poems which were collected in *Khulhe Asmani Rang*. For properly understanding these sky coloured poems one needs either complete seclusion or self-experience of witnessing the thick shades of close-grown forest trees where even a single ray of sunlight dare not penetrate.

These poems remain still unpublished. He writes, "Only here I have been able to comprehend that the moon, sun, human beings, animals, and birds are all bound together in one life by the minute silky strings of love."

The bubbling life-unity was on its increase in his heart. Through his visible and physical fellow-beings, he rose to the realization of the imperceptible which ultimately resulted in witnessing the pure and real helarity. Sitting in his upper floor room, he kept himself busy in writing. Sometimes while writing, he used to come down in the courtyard where about fifty tenants were putting up. The moment he came down, all animals including bulls, cows, buffaloes and goats turned their faces towards him. Every animal became restless and desired his close attention as his hands used to be brimmed with breads. To some he gave bread, of others he itched their necks politely and the remaining ones were hugged by him. It used to be a wonderful occasion. The small kids and children of these families used to run to him and cling with his legs and hands. He had also prepared their movie-film which unfortunately has been left in Pakistan.

He has given a wonderful description of the unity of this Baar - area:

> The dumb trees
> Having drunk from the kisses of the North wind,
> Come to have,
> Millions of tongues.

One day Bego's sister complained to Swamiji's mother, "Oh mother, I have seen with my own eyes, your Sardar was kissing the flowers of an acacia tree."

It was November 1928 and he was completely absorbed with his poems for *Khulhe Asmani Rang*, when we received a letter from Dehradun informing us that Gargi had been blessed with a daughter through caesarean operation, but the child and her mother were perfectly safe. He forgot all his engagements. He hired a tonga and reached Jarranwala and then left for Dehradun. He was very much upset in his mind, apprehending that he might not be able to see Gargi alive. Suppressed by such dreadful apprehensions, he reached our bungalow 'Ivango' and cried, " Where is my daughter?" I pacified him that Gargi and her daughter were perfectly alright and they were still in the hospital, where we would go after some time. The servant came and said, "Sir, water for your bath is ready. Kindly have your bath." He scolded him and angrily said, "Why did you utter this nonsense? Do you think I am in a mood to have a bath?" The servant knowing his temperament kept silent. Then he brought tea for him. He kicked the table furiously throwing away the tea pot and the cup saucer. "I want to go to the hospital immediately. After satisfying myself about her safe and sound health, only then I can think of having a bath and a cup of tea."

Somebody advised me that he should meet Gargi in a normal way. But I did not dare to suggest to him. "Who can instruct the Lord for his actions?" I replied. He got ready to accompany me to the hospital. Before leaving he ordered the gardener to arrange a basket of beautiful blossomed flowers. He took the basket and went to the hospital in a joyful mood. "Where is my Gargi?" Gargi was overjoyed with pleasure for she apprehended that her father might express his displeasure over her giving birth to a daughter. The nurses brought the infant child from the other room. Seeing his grand-daughter, he was so overwhelmed with joy that he gave a hundred rupee note to the nurses to go and have sweets.

After two nights, when we all were asleep, I heard the beating of shoes. I woke up immediately and was surprised to see that he was beating the floor with his shoe.

"What are you doing?" I asked. He said, "In my dream my late grand-father had come to take Gargi. I was turning him out." Hearing that I felt like laughing. Inspite of my best efforts I could not control my laughter. I had fears that he would be enraged over my laughing but contrary to my apprehension, he also joined me in it. After a month and a half, Gargi was discharged from the hospital. He christened Gargi's daughter `Anila.' Her father-in-law and mother-in-law came to see her. When they were planning for their return journey, Swamiji asked them, "When do you intend to reach Lyalpur?"

They said, "First of all we will go to Haridwar and then we intend to go to Mastuana to meet the saint. After that we will go to Kartarpur for selecting the swinging-columns. We will go back to Lyalpur via Amritsar".

When Swamiji heard their programme, he smiled.

His last Days

It is as difficult to give expression to his thoughts and views as it is to express God's form and colour in words. Whatever he said or did was never calculated. Like a child he was always lisping. His only concern was to judge the reaction of the person he was talking to. If somebody expressed his liking for the topic about which he was talking, he used to continue his discourse on the subject. But if the listener passed on his views to others, generally the tone and temper got changed. When this changed version of his views reached him back through a third party, he was perplexed and shocked over their changed character.

Ultimately he started worrying about these things.

Moreover, he could not overcome his worry that even his life-companion and close-relatives had misunderstood him and in a way he was responsible for their confusion and misunderstanding. When he noticed a change in the life of persons for whom he had lived, he got an unbearable mental shock and felt shattered. Being a sensitive poet, his heart was always full of emotions and sentiments. Just like innocent children, he used to forget his worries for a moment, when somebody had a word of praise for him. He would laugh and play with others. His heart was just like a crystal gem which could not avoid the reflection of others. It is impossible to find another living person like him on this earth. His agonies and comforts were always short-lived and transitory. His anger was like thick clouds which burst into severe rain with a thunder and then clear the sky. But he could not forget his inner-worry and started preparing himself for leaving this world for good. I tried to pacify and console him to my maximum capacity and ability but it seemed to have little effect on him. He got angry with himself and started thinking himself to be worthless. There was a sea-change in his temperament. His thundering voice, bursting anger and blossoming smiles, all forsook him. In this disturbed state of mind, he wrote an essay in Panjabi, giving vent to his perturbed feelings, and sent it for publication. He anxiously awaited its seeing the light of the day, but months passed by and it could not come out in print. He left this world and it was never published. We have not been able to trace that essay so far.

Those who had enjoyed his loud laughs were wonder struck to see him silent and mum. Earlier his eyes were always ready to shed tears at the slightest inspiration or disturbance. Visualizing that everlasting form of Power, he used to sing:

> Beautiful to look at but with empty hands
> What can you expect from idols?
> Prepare at least a rosary with eyebrow,
> Strung with pearls of tears.

But now his dry-eyes were like drought-bitten lands which had never enjoyed the fortune of water-shedding clouds. From Dehradun he went to Panjab because he was to visit his farmland for depositing his land-revenue in the government treasury. On his way he dropped at Lahore. Despair had completely occupied and over-shadowed him. To some he did disclose a little of his despair but to many he did not tell anything. Crippled with despair and depression he sang:

> Oh God, I am fed up with the assemblage of this world
> How can one enjoy the warmth of a meeting with a crippled heart?

He could not come into contact with any exuberant person who might have fanned his extinguishing fire of will and pleasure into a full fledged flame. A person always gladdened with mirth and pleasure was being engulfed by despair and depression so much that he forgot his old habits of playing, singing and eating. The letters that I received from him at Dehradun were full of sadness and sorrow.

In the beginning of November 1930, we received the sad news that he was suffering from tuberculosis. Hearing this I began trembling. Even Dr. Khudadad, who was known for his self-control and self-discipline, felt shattered and turned pale. Dr. Balbir Singh got worried and confounded.

I took my second son Nirlep Singh with me and left for Lyalpur where Gargi and Malik Amar Singh were living. Reaching there I found that he was playing with his grand-daughter Anila.

I said, "Let us go to Dehradun." But he did not reply to my suggestion. Rather he said, "Bring my books and manuscripts from the farms."

Myself, Nirlep Singh and Malik Amar Singh left for the farms and brought all his manuscripts but we did not touch anything else.

I brought him to Dehradun in the end of November 1930. But he had become allergic to this city and its city-dwellers. He was not feeling at home at Dehradun. So we decided to shift to Dohiwala which was about twelve miles away. There was a factory and a river nearby. The factory was doing very well. He felt happy for having shifted to this place. All the servants, workers and machinemen who had earlier worked under him used to come to him for consultation. He guided them whenever there was a problem. Most of the day he had a stroll in the garden and felt happy.

The disease had compelled him to behave and talk like a child. He once said, "Look Maya, I have a tassel entwined on my head and finger-tips on my feet which create music. Do you hear their sound?"

I said, "Yes, I can listen to it."

He generally played with the children living at Dohiwale.

But his inner will to live was withering. He was like a plant whose roots, except one, had dried up. I tried my level best to see to it that his dried roots got established at their right place, but it seemed that he had got completely annoyed with himself.

His body went on melting but his mind was still saturated with the spirit of unity and love. He had neither grudge against anybody nor anger for anyone.

He was under the medical treatment of doctors from Dehradun who used to come daily to Dohiwale to check him. Dr. Khudadad and Dr. Balbir Singh also occassionally visited him along with other friends. From 1905 till his death, Dr. Khudadad lived with us.

When it was realised that Dohiwala's surroundings had not helped him in any way in improving his heath, we shifted to Dehradun where a fresh medical check up was conducted. Even his lung-functioning was temporarily stopped, but there was no improvement.

He used to talk to Dr. Khudadad mostly about his farm-land. Payment of its land-revenue was a constant source of worry for him for he feared that by non-payment, the land might be confiscated. Though at that time we were very hard up financially, yet Dr. Khudadad remitted the revenue-money to relieve him of his worry. When he saw the revenue-payment receipt with his own eyes, he felt happy.

Soon there were symptoms of other diseases in him such as gout, albramedaria, diabetes apart from tuberculosis. He went for his x-ray but the doctors failed to understand how a person with such wide ribs, could suffer from tuberculosis. His ribs wer wider than an inch. But nobody knew that his main illness was his inner-despair and depression. He did not object to any sort of treatment. His response to their treatment was always forthcoming as if his body had become benumbed. At the time of temporary stoppage lung-functioning, he remained calm and quiet. He did not utter a word of complaint even at the extraction of a huge quantity of blood.

In March 1930 he had received a letter from Damodar Singh engineer with whom he had travelled to Japan and had been his room-mate for three years. He had written that Saint Lakhbir Singh be requested for praying for his recovery.

He summoned Dr. Balbir Singh from the adjoining room. As he was unable to speak in his normal voice, Dr. Balbir Singh took his ear very close to his mouth.

He said, "Don't request the saint for my recovery." Touching his arm, he said, "It is not proper to request for praying for this small perishable body. You are not to do that. Let His will to happen".

He used to worry greatly at my slightest indisposition. "Maya, if you fall ill, who will look after me?" he would say. He had great fears about my health. He was well aware of the fact that he had developed a contagious disease. So he took special precautions to avoid other people's company. But in his lifetime he had no reservation for persons suffering from infectious diseases. Much before his becoming a T.B. patient, he had been visiting the hospital at Lahore to enquire about the health of a T.B. patient, Bibi Gobind Kaur - who is still living. He used to sit by her side talking and even hug her often.

I also had no reservation for this infectious disease. Day and night I was by his side. As usual before going to bed we continued exchanging good-night greetings by embracing and loving each other.

He used to ask me, "Please don't do that". But I always replied, "I cannot waste these invaluable moments for the sake of this perishable body. It is a tonic for me. You are not to worry please."

Before his journey for the heavenly abode, he expressed a desire to meet Sardar Sampuran Singh, Barrister. In those days he had gone abroad. But luckily he returned to India and alongwith his wife Narinder Kaur, he came to see Swamiji. They embraced each other very dearly. Though their eyes were full of tears, yet they tried their level best not to shed them in his presence. They took meals together. He talked to his brother Sampuran Singh and his sister Narinder Kaur (wife of Sampuran Singh) for hours together. Then they left for Lyalpur. During his illness, he did not express his desire of meeting anyone else. But one day he remembered civil surgeon Dewan Singh. He had quarrelled with him long long ago over some issue. During that quarrel, Dr. Dewan Singh had felt hurt and enraged, So Swamiji thought of straightening those strained relations with him. He got a letter written to Dr. Dewan Singh. When Dr. Dewan Singh came to meet him, both of them embraced each other with love and affection. Swamiji requested him "My dear friend, kindly pardon me for my lapses." Dr. Dewan Singh again embraced him and said, "Oh dear brother, do you still remember that quarrel? Now forget it." Dr. Dewan Singh wept bitterly and left for Simla the same night.

One day before leaving this world for good, I was sitting all alone beside him. He said, "Maya, I am very sorry for not leaving enough money for you." I was surprised to hear such words from him. I consoled him and said, "How is it that this idea has come to you? The amount of wealth that you have bestowed upon me, is much more and of greater value than the money that a king leaves for his queen. You have satisfied me so much that I have won over the feeling of hunger. I don't want anything! Please don't have any worry on that count."

I did not wish that he should be entwined with emotions in any way at this critical juncture of his life. I kept on my movements and actions as normal as I possibly could.

The doctor called me to another room and said, "This great personality is leaving this world for his heavenly abode. The heart has stopped functioning, only his lungs are active."

I felt as if my bones were shattered into pieces. As at the time of an earthquake the beams of the roof fall down with a thud, I also felt the breaking of my back-bone. I went to the room of *Guru Granth Sahib* and praying for his deliverance, said, "Oh my Guru Nanak, please come to my rescue, hold me so that I don't falter at this critical moment of my life. He is coming to you. Bestow me with the power to send him the gifts of *bani* (hymns)." After uttering all this, I felt a sort of complete tranquility in my mind. I came to his room and sat beside him.

He said, "Maya call brother Dr. Khudadad. He was in the adjacent room pacing about in a bewildered mind. He came and stood by his side silently.

He said, "Dear brother, I am going".

"No, no, please don't say that," requested Khudadad.

He lifted his long arm with a swing and said, "You will always say like this."

I thought that this arm which had swung many a time during his lectures to others and had left a lasting effect on their hearts might have been raised by him for the last time. The speciality of Khudadad's personality was that he did not take to his heart anything tragic or painful. He quietly went out.

Swamiji again repeated, "Maya, I am going."

I did not want to bind him with the affection-string at the last leg of his life and so I uttered these words of Guru's hymns:

> Oh Nanak, bestowed with His name
> You may go to heaven with credit.

He closed his eyes after uttering his last words. He was still breathing. I stamped an affection-kiss on his forehead. But he nodded his head as a sign of disapproval.

In that room many amorists of *Bani* (hymns) like my mother, my sister and two nieces were present.

I was reciting *Bawan Akhri* and his hand was within my mild hand-grip for feeling his pulse.

While listening to the hymns, his pulse slowed down and he became complete silent and mute. It seemed.

> As water loses its form and existence while mixing with other water.

> Similarly the human spirit intermingles with the God Almighty.

It was afternoon. The room was creating a strange and miraculous effect. There was no feeling of separation. Rather it was creating an atmosphere of union and oneness.

On the evening of March 31, 1931 his dead body was cremated. The atmosphere of the whole house was calm and peaceful. All were reciting the *Bani* (hymns). The whole family had assembled on that occasion. The inner atmosphere of the home can be described in the words of Kabir:

> After the day of death
> Bliss prevails every where,
>
> I have become intuned with my God,
> My companions are remembering the Lord.

Dohiwala   Maya Puran Singh
1-12-1962